THE UNITED NATIONS AND POPULATION

Major Resolutions and Instruments

THE UNITED NATIONS AND POPULATION

Major Resolutions and Instruments

published in cooperation with the
United Nations Fund for Population Activities

1974
OCEANA PUBLICATIONS, INC. — DOBBS FERRY, NEW YORK
A. W. SIJTHOFF — LEIDEN

760869

This volume is No. 7 in the Law and Population Book Series published by the Law and Population Programme. For information on earlier volumes, write to: The Director, Law and Population Programme, Fletcher School of Law and Diplomacy, Tufts University, Medford, Massachusetts 02155.

Library of Congress Cataloging in Publication Data
Main entry under title:

The United Nations and population: major resolutions
  and instruments.

1. Population. 2. United Nations. 3. Social
policy. I. United Nations Fund for Population Activities.

HB871.U56   301.32   74-9637
ISBN 0-379-00031-8 (Oceana)
ISBN 90-286-0454-5 (Sijthoff)

1974 will be World Population Year, and it is essential that mankind takes this opportunity to make real progress towards determining the complex problems which face it, and how best they can be resolved. The The United Nations World Population Conference, to be held in Bucharest, Romania, in August 1974 will be the first world-wide inter-governmental conference on this important and difficult subject, and this meeting emphasises the fact that the problems of population are global, and require global understanding and action.

In our interdependent world, it is not possible nor practicable to attempt to solve problems in isolation. Thus, matters of population must be seen in conjunction with many other factors — including health, education, employment, food supplies, housing, and environment. This Compendium — which was originated by the International Advisory Committee on Population and Law — emphasises this dominant fact very clearly, and it reminds us of the unique capacity of the United Nations to bring together government, non-governmental organizations, and interested citizens from all over the world to co-operate in resolving the long-term problems of mankind.

In commending this publication, I wish to express my personal gratitude to all who have contributed to its preparation.

PREFACE

This volume is dedicated to the World Population Year.

Published in three official languages of the United Nations — English, French and Spanish — the present volume comprises, as its title indicates, the major resolutions and instruments of the various United Nations bodies having a bearing on population. The selection of materials is guided by: (a) the intrinsic importance of the resolutions; (b) the existence of any novel features in the resolutions; (c) the usefulness of the resolutions in providing guidelines for national legislation and programmes; (d) the comprehensiveness of coverage; (e) the need for a balanced presentation in terms of subject matter and geographical regions; and (f) the relevancy of the resolutions to current United Nations activities and programmes. Repetitive or non-substantive resolutions, as well as detailed reports and documents of the various United Nations bodies, are therefore omitted.

Familiarity with the organization of the present volume may well facilitate the reader's search for material. In the first place, two tables of contents are provided, one brief, the other annotated. Both are arranged according to the organizations concerned and in chronological order.

Second, the narrower prevails over the broader; the text of a General Assembly resolution relating to a subordinate organ is placed under the latter organ instead of the parent body.

Third, the texts of the various United Nations Declarations and Proclamations are grouped with Conventions, even if adopted as General Assembly resolutions (cross references are given).

Fourth, the cut-off date for material to be included in this volume is 18 May 1973.

The completion of this volume would not have been possible without the collaboration of many individuals and organizations. In a very real sense, the volume symbolizes the finest inter-agency co-operation dedicated to the common goal of making the United Nations concern with the population problem as widely known as possible.

Originally begun as a project on "The United Nations and Population: Principal Documents" by Luke T. Lee, Executive Secretary of the International Advisory Committee on Population and Law (a non-governmental organization in consultative status with ECOSOC), it has evolved into a publication prepared by the United Nations Fund for Population Activities with the assistance of the United Nations Centre for Economic and Social Information, the Population Division, and the Centre for Social and Humanitarian Matters.

In addition to constituting a basic source of reference to United Nations resolutions and instruments concerning population, it serves as a telling reminder that the concern of the United Nations system — and hence also of its Member States — is not limited to the statistical or demographic aspects of population, but extends indeed to the whole spectrum of problems confronting each individual human being: health, aging, food, housing, work, marriage, education, migration, environment, discrimination, privacy, etc. These problems are viewed not only from the perspective of adult men and women, but also from that of the child, whose needs as a human being have heretofore been regarded as mere appendages of those of his parents. The fact that States with differing political, ideological and economic systems can be united in focusing their attention on the advancement of individual well-being as a basic human right is eloquent proof of the existence of a United Nations. For, in the final analysis, the State is made up of individuals, and the competition among the different systems in promoting individual well-being as a shared concern cannot fail to exert a salutary impact upon the dignity of man as well as on the issue of war and peace.

TABLE OF CONTENTS

[An Annotated Table of Contents follows immediately
upon this table]

II. Conventions, Declarations and Proclamations *(continued)*

III. **General Assembly Resolutions**

III. General Assembly Resolutions *(continued)*

III. General Assembly Resolutions (*continued*)

VII. The Specialized Agencies

(Order of documents is chronological under
chapter and organizational headings)

II. Conventions, Declarations and Proclamations *(continued)*

II. Conventions, Declarations and Proclamations *(continued)*

II. Conventions, Declarations and Proclamations *(continued)*

appropriate assistance from the rest of the world community, family planning, raising the level of employment, development of education, the provision of improved housing, health services, etc.]

Adopted by the United Nations Conference on the Human Environment, 1972.
[In its Declaration, the Conference calls upon Governments and peoples to exert common efforts for the preservation and improvement of the human environment and lays down a set of principles to guide the peoples of the world in the preservation and enhancement of that environment. It notes *inter alia* the problems presented for the environment by the growth of population and the need for the application of demographic policies where such problems exist.]

Adopted at the Second Asian Population Conference, 1972.
[In its Declaration the Conference recognizes the right of every couple to determine the number and spacing of their children and the social and economic impact of individual family size on societies. It emphasizes the urgency of problems of population growth and declares that integrated national planning and coordinated action are required at the highest government level. It lists the various ways in which the Governments of the region should carry out their population policies and programmes.]

III. General Assembly Resolutions

III. General Assembly Resolutions (*continued*)

III. General Assembly Resolutions *(continued)*

III. General Assembly Resolutions *(continued)*

III. General Assembly Resolutions *(continued)*

> elderly and the aged is expected to deteriorate
> in many countries unless appropriate policies are
> initiated to deal with their needs and requests
> the Secretary-General to continue the study of
> the changing socio-economic and cultural role of
> the aged and to prepare a report suggesting
> guidelines for action related to their needs.]

IV. Economic and Social Council

A. *Council Resolutions*

Economic and Social Council resolution 104 (VI).
[The resolution endorses the conclusions of the
United Nations Conference on Trade and Employment (1948) relating to the need to achieve and
maintain full employment and economic stability.]

Economic and Social Council resolution 156 (VII).
[The resolution allocates functions as to migration
as between the Population Commission and the
Social Commission and defines their respective
responsibilities in this field.]

Economic and Social Council resolution 222 (IX).
[The resolution requests the Secretary-General to
invite the Administrative Committee on Coordination
to set up a Technical Assistance Board (TAB) to
participate in the Expanded Programme of Technical
Assistance guided by a statement of principles attached to the resolution. The guiding principles provide a framework for the provision of advisory services at the request of Governments.]

Economic and Social Council resolution 471 (XV).
[The resolution endorses the decision of the Population Commission to concentrate its efforts in three

IV. Economic and Social Council (*continued*)

A. *Council Resolutions (continued)*

areas: (1) studies of the interrelationships of demographic, economic and social factors; (2) analysis of further population trends; and (3) studies of migration, both international and internal. It also asks the Secretary-General to give technical assistance to Governments in the preparation of analytical studies of their census results.]

Economic and Social Council resolution 571 (XIX). [The resolution endorses the Population Commission's proposal for a programme of studies on "population trends and their relation to economic and social factors, especially in the development of the less-developed countries".]

Economic and Social Council resolution 642 (XXIII). [The resolution recognizes the "direct relationship between the problems of population and economic and social developments", and calls for studies of means of improving census and vital statistics in Africa and of the establishment of demographic training and research centres in Africa.]

Economic and Social Council resolution 721 (XXVII).
[The resolution requests the Secretary-General to make United Nations assistance available to under-developed countries in carrying out demographic pilot studies and other projects demonstrating the value of utilizing demographic data including the results of censuses. It also asks the Secretary-General to develop studies of internal migration in relation to economic and social development.]

Economic and Social Council resolution 820 B (XXXI).

IV. Economic and Social Council *(continued)*

    A. *Council Resolutions (continued)*

IV. Economic and Social Council *(continued)*

A. *Council Resolutions (continued)*

their various programmes in the field of population and invites UNESCO to pursue its education, social sciences and mass media in this regard.]

Economic and Social Council resolution 1326 (XLIV).
[The Economic and Social Council notes the various services offered in family planning programmes which have important implications for women and invites interested Governments to undertake national surveys on the status of women and family planning.]

Economic and Social Council resolution 1347 (XLV).
[The resolution recognizes the importance of giving appropriate attention to the interrelations of economic, social and demographic factors in formulating development programmes and requests the Secretary-General *inter alia* to pursue a programme of work covering training research, information and advisory services in the various population fields, and to give special attention to developing those aspects of work in those fields which directly benefit developing countries.]

Economic and Social Council resolution 1483 (XLVIII).
[The resolution calls upon the Preparatory Committee for the Second United Nations Development Decade to consider including in its development strategy a text noting that efforts to promote economic and social development in the Second

IV. Economic and Social Council *(continued)*

A. *Council Resolutions (continued)*

United Nations Development Decade could be frustrated by the continuance of the present high rates of population growth and that national policies aimed at reducing such growth should be regarded as among the essential aspects of development strategy.]

Economic and Social Council resolution 1484 (XLVIII).
[The resolution approves the proposal that a World Population Conference should be held under the auspices of the United Nations in 1974.]

Economic and Social Council resolution 1486 (XLVIII).
[The resolution calls upon all States Members of the United Nations to participate in the 1970 World Population Census Programme and to develop their vital statistics in accordance with the proposed World Programme for Improvement of Vital Statistics, and urges Governments of States Members to give full attention to population programmes in development planning and in policy-making. It requests the Secretary-General *inter alia* to promote the 1970 round of population censuses and to conduct a second inquiry among Governments concerning population trends, economic and social development, and the policies and action programmes of those Governments.]

Economic and Social Council resolution 1564 (L).
[The resolution requests the Secretary-General to publish "Principles and recommendations for a

IV. Economic and Social Council *(continued)*

A. *Council Resolutions (continued)*
vital statistics system", to give them wide distribution, and to give assistance to developing countries in the implementation of those principles and
recommendations.]

22. POPULATION AND DEVELOPMENT (1972)   123

Economic and Social Council resolution 1672 (LII).
[The resolution urges Member States to give full
attention to their demographic objectives during
the biennial review of the Second United Nations
Development Decade, to cooperate in achieving a
reduction of the rate of population growth in
countries whose rate of growth is too high, and
to ensure that information and education about
family planning are made available to all by the
end of the Decade. It endorses the draft programme for the 1974 World Population Conference and decides to assign to the Population Commission the function of the preparatory body for
Conference and the World Population Year, and
to place on the agenda of the World Population
Conference a draft World Population Plan of Action. It also approves the programme for the
World Population Year, 1974 and calls for active
participation in the World Population Year activities. It endorses the five-year and two-year population programmes recommended by the Population Commission and requests the Secretary-
General to take various measures in pursuance of
the programme of work recommended by the
Commission.]

23. STATUS OF THE UNMARRIED MOTHER (1972)   128

Economic and Social Council resolution 1679 (LII).
[The resolution recommends that all States that
have not yet done so should eliminate any existing
social discrimination against an unmarried mother
and her child; it recommends a number of general
principles for achieving that end.]

V. Regional Economic Commissions

[The Conference invites Members of ECAFE to
take account of the urgency of adopting a positive
population policy related to their needs. It asks
for the facilitation of direct exchange of information among Governments on all aspects of population and social and economic growth and the expansion of the scope of technical assistance in
the region. It recommends a number of general
principles for the formulation and implementation
of national policies and international cooperation
in demographic work. It also stresses the need to
step up agricultural production. Noting that there
have been rapid reductions in mortality without
corresponding reductions in fertility, it makes
recommendations to deal with this problem. In
view of the degree of urbanization throughout the
region, it recommends a number of social welfare
services. The Conference notes the relationship
between population growth and the development
of education and recommends that ECAFE should
include in its activities such studies as the effects
of education upon population trends. It also emphasizes the need for the improvement of vital
statistics.]

V. Regional Economic Commissions *(continued)*

B. *Economic Commission for Asia and the Far East (continued)*

adopt family planning measures aimed at the achievement of more desirable rates of population growth.]

C. *Economic Commission for Latin America (ECLA)*

Resolution of the Economic Commission for Latin America 187 (IX).
[The resolution recommends that the regional demographic programmes of the United Nations be intensified, and asks the ECLA secretariat to offer assistance to Governments in making use of the findings of population censuses.]

Resolution of the Economic Commission for Latin America 290 (XIII).
[The resolution recommends that the ECLA secretariat should give special attention *inter alia* to the study of national policies for regional development, taking into account the problems of population concentration in urban areas and to the continuation of demographic studies in order to shed more light on population problems.]

Resolution of the Economic Commission for Latin America 310 (XIV).
[The resolution recommends that Governments of developing countries, members of ECLA, should

V. Regional Economic Commissions *(continued)*

   C. *Economic Commissions for Latin America (ECLA) (continued)*

define their economic and social development goals and objectives for the decade, strengthen and develop planning systems, adopt measures to improve their statistical services, and make available on a regular basis basic statistical data for employment, income distribution, urban and rural levels of living, etc.]

Resolution of the Economic Commission for Latin America 327 (XV).
[The resolution approves proposals for strengthening demographic information and research in Latin America and urges the ECLA secretariat to strengthen its capacity to assist Governments in improving demographic statistics and including demographic variables in development planning.]

   D. *Economic Commission for Africa (ECA)*

Resolution of the Economic Commission for Africa 230 (X).
[The Conference of Ministers calls upon the Executive Secretary to speed up the establishment of sub-regional demographic training centres, to study the relations between population and socio-economic development, and prepare a demographic manual for Africa.]

   E. *Economic Commission for Western Asia (ECWA)*

VI. Other United Nations Bodies *(continued)*

C. *United Nations Children's Fund
(UNICEF) (continued)*

for the protection of the child and the urgent
need for continuing the work of UNICEF, particularly in the under-developed regions of the
world, reaffirms the pertinent provisions of
General Assembly resolutions 57 (I) and 417 (V)
with the exception of any reference to time-limits.]

UNICEF Executive Board Resolution, 1966.
[The resolution requests the advice of the
UNICEF/WHO Joint Committee on Health Policy
on the best way in which UNICEF might participate in family planning programmes, with particular reference to the technical aspects.]

UNICEF Executive Board Decision, 1967.
[The Executive Board recognizes the need
for rapid expansion of health services to provide
scope for family planning as an integral part of
such services.]

D. *United Nations Fund for Population
Activities (UNFPA)*

General Assembly resolution 2815 (XXVI).
[The resolution notes the progress made by the
Fund and requests the Secretary-General to take
steps to achieve desired improvements in the
machinery of the Fund for the expeditious
delivery of population programmes, including
measures for the recruitment and training of
experts and personnel.]

VII. The Specialized Agencies *(continued)*

A. *International Labour Organization (ILO) (continued)*

Adopted by the ILO General Conference, 1955.
[The Recommendation calls for measures to discourage migratory movements when considered
undesirable in the interests of the migrant
workers and for the protection of migrant workers
during the period of their employment.]

[The General Conference invites the Governing
Body of the International Labour Office to request
the Director-General to undertake a comprehensive study on the influence of rapid population
growth on opportunities for training and employment and on the welfare of workers, and to
submit proposals to the Governing Body on
further action that might be taken by the ILO.]

Adopted by the ILO Governing Body, 1968.

[The conclusions state what action developing
countries should take to raise the standard of
living of the working population and note that
rapid population growth in many developing
countries is giving rise to serious employment
problems, and that due attention should be paid
to the adoption of population policies and to the
introduction of family planning programmes.]

VII. The Specialized Agencies (*continued*)

FAO Conference resolution 1/67.
[The Conference recognizes that substantial improvement must be brought about in agricultural
production, processing, etc. if the needs of
developing countries are to be met, concurs in
the need for organizational improvements in FAO,
and decides *inter alia* to move forward with the
appointment of full-time Country Representatives
with over-all responsibility for FAO programmes
within their respective countries.]

[The General Conference notes the need for including instruction on population questions in
school courses and of family planning in all
relevant curricula, invites the Director-General
to cooperate furhter wtih organizations by offering UNESCO's services within the fields of
population and family planning with special emphasis on their socio-cultural implications and

VII. The Specialized Agencies (*continued*)

D. *World Health Organization (WHO) (continued)*

1

PART ONE

CHARTER OF THE UNITED NATIONS

PART I.
CHARTER OF THE UNITED NATIONS

WE THE PEOPLES
OF THE UNITED NATIONS
DETERMINED

. . .

to reaffirm faith in fundamental human rights, in the dignity and worth of the human person, in the equal rights of men and women and of nations large and small, and . . .

to promote social progress and better standards of life in larger freedom,

AND FOR THESE ENDS

to employ international machinery for the promotion of the economic and social advancement of all peoples,

HAVE RESOLVED TO
COMBINE OUR EFFORTS TO
ACCOMPLISH THESE AIMS

Accordingly, our respective Governments, through representatives assembled in the city of San Francisco, who have exhibited their full powers found to be in good and due form, have agreed to the present Charter of the United Nations and do hereby establish an international organization to be known as the United Nations.

CHAPTER I
PURPOSES AND PRINCIPLES

Article 1

The Purposes of the United Nations are:

. . .

3. To achieve international cooperation in solving international problems of an economic, social, cultural, or humanitarian character, and in promoting and encouraging respect for human rights and for fundamental freedoms for all without distinction as to race, sex, language, or religion; and

4. To be a centre for harmonizing the actions of nations in the attainment of these common ends.

Article 2

. . .

2. All Members, in order to ensure to all of them the rights and benefits resulting from membership, shall fulfill in good faith the obligations assumed by them in accordance with the present Charter . . .

7. Nothing contained in the present Charter shall authorize the United Nations to intervene in matters which are essentially within the domestic jurisdiction of any state . . .

CHAPTER IV
THE GENERAL ASSEMBLY

. . .

Functions and Powers

Article 10

The General Assembly may discuss any questions or any matters within the scope of the present Charter or relating to the powers and functions of any organs provided for in the present Charter, and, except as provided in Article 12, may make recommendations to the Members of the United Nations or to the Security Council or to both on any such questions or matters.

. . .

Article 13

1. The General Assembly shall initiate studies and make recommendations for the purpose of:

. . .

b. promoting international cooperation in the economic, social, cultural, educational, and health fields, and assisting in the realization of human rights and fundamental freedoms for all without distinction as to race, sex, language, or religion.

2. The further responsibilities, functions and powers of the General Assembly with respect to matters mentioned in paragraph 1(b) above are set forth in Chapters IX and X.

. . .

CHAPTER IX
INTERNATIONAL ECONOMIC AND SOCIAL COOPERATION

Article 55

With a view to the creation of conditions of stability and well-being which are necessary for peaceful and friendly relations among nations based on respect for the principle of equal rights and self-determination of peoples, the United Nations shall promote:

a. higher standards of living, full employment, and conditions of economic and social progress and development;

b. solutions of international economic, social, health, and related problems; and international cultural and educational cooperation; and

c. universal respect for, and observance of, human rights and fundamental freedoms for all without distinction as to race, sex, language, or religion.

Article 56

All Members pledge themselves to take joint and separate action in cooperation with the Organization for the achievement of the purposes set forth in Article 55.

Article 57

1. The various specialized agencies, established by intergovernmental agreement and having wide international responsibilities, as defined in their basic instruments, in economic, social, cultural, educational, health, and related fields, shall be brought into relationship with the United Nations in accordance with the provisions of Article 63.

2. Such agencies thus brought into relationship with the United Nations are hereinafter referred to as specialized agencies.

Article 58

The Organization shall make recommendations for the coordination of the policies and activities of the specialized agencies.

Article 59

The Organization shall, where appropriate, initiate negotiations among the states concerned for the creation of any new specialized agencies required for the accomplishment of the purposes set forth in Article 55.

Article 60

Responsibility for the discharge of the functions of the Organization set forth in this Chapter shall be vested in the General Assembly and, under the authority of the General Assembly, in the Economic and Social Council, which shall have for this purpose the powers set forth in Chapter X.

CHAPTER X
THE ECONOMIC AND SOCIAL COUNCIL

Composition

Article 61[1]

1. The Economic and Social Council shall consist of twenty-seven Members of the United Nations elected by the General Assembly.

2. . . . . nine members of the Economic and Social Council shall be elected each year for a term of three years. A retiring member shall be eligible for immediate re-election.

. . .

Functions and Powers

Article 62

1. The Economic and Social Council may make or initiate studies and reports with respect to international economic, social, cultural, educational, health, and related matters and may make recommendations with respect to any such matters to the General Assembly, to the Members of the United Nations, and to the specialized agencies concerned.

2. It may make recommendations for the purpose of promoting respect for, and observance of, human rights and fundamental freedoms for all.

3. It may prepare draft conventions for submission to the General Assembly, with respect to matters falling within its competence.

4. It may call, in accordance with the rules prescribed by the United Nations, international conferences on matters falling within its competence.

Article 63

1. The Economic and Social Council may enter into agreements with any of the agencies referred to in Article 57, defining the terms on which the agency concerned shall be brought into relationship with the United Nations. Such agreements shall be subject to approval by the General Assembly.

2. It may coordinate the activities of the specialized agencies through consultation with and recommendations to such agencies and through recommendations to the General Assembly and to the Members of the United Nations.

Article 64

1. The Economic and Social Council may take appropriate steps to obtain regular reports from the specialized agencies. It may make arrange-

[1]Amended text of Article 61, which came into force on 31 August 1965.

ments with the Members of the United Nations and with the specialized agencies to obtain reports on the steps taken to give effect to its own recommendations and to recommendations on matters falling within its competence made by the General Assembly.

2. It may communicate its observations on these reports to the General Assembly.

Article 66

1. The Economic and Social Council shall perform such functions as fall within its competence in connection with the carrying out of the recommendations of the General Assemb .

2. It may, with the approval of the General Assembly, perform services at the request of Members of the United Nations and at the request of specialized agencies.

3. It shall perform such other functions as are specified elsewhere in the present Charter as may be assigned to it by the General Assembly.

Procedure

Article 68

The Economic and Social Council shall set up commissions in economic and social fields and for the promotion of human rights, and such other commissions as may be required for the performance of its functions.

. . .

Article 69

The Economic and Social Council shall invite any Member of the United Nations to participate, without vote, in its deliberations on any matter of particular concern to that Member.

Article 70

The Economic and Social Council may make arrangements for representatives of the specialized agencies to participate, without vote, in its deliberations and in those of the commissions established by it, and for its representatives to participate in the deliberations of the specialized agencies.

Article 71

The Economic and Social Council may make suitable arrangements for consultation with non-governmental organizations which are concerned with matters within its competence. Such arrangements may be made with international organizations and, where appropriate, with national organizations after consultation with the Member of the United Nations concerned.

. . .

PART TWO

CONVENTIONS, DECLARATIONS AND PROCLAMATIONS

CONVENTIONS, DECLARATIONS AND PROCLAMATIONS

1. CONVENTION ON THE PREVENTION AND PUNISHMENT OF THE CRIME OF GENOCIDE[1]

The Contracting Parties,

Having considered the declaration made by the General Assembly of the United Nations in its resolution 96 (I) dated 11 December 1946 that genocide is a crime under international law, contrary to the spirit and aims of the United Nations and condemned by the civilized world,

Recognizing that at all periods of history genocide has inflicted great losses on humanity, and

Being convinced that, in order to liberate mankind from such an odious scourge, international co-operation is required,

Hereby agree as hereinafter provided.

Article I

The Contracting Parties confirm that genocide, whether committed in time of peace or in time of war, is a crime under international law which they undertake to prevent and to punish.

Article II

In the present Convention, genocide means any of the following acts committed with intent to destroy, in whole or in part, a national, ethnical, racial or religious group, as such:

(a) Killing members of the group;

(b) Causing serious bodily or mental harm to members of the group;

(c) Deliberately inflicting on the group conditions of life calculated to bring about its physical destruction in whole or in part;

(d) Imposing measures intended to prevent births within the group;

(e) Forcibly transferring children of the group to another group.

Article III

The following acts shall be punishable:

(a) Genocide;

---

[1]Approved and proposed for signature and ratification or accession by the General Assembly in its resolution 260 A (III) of 9 December 1948. Came into force 12 January 1951.

(b) Conspiracy to commit genocide;

(c) Direct and public incitement to commit genocide;

(d) Attempt to commit genocide;

(e) Complicity in genocide.

Article IV

Persons committing genocide or any of the other acts enumerated in article III shall be punished, whether they are constitutionally responsible rulers, public officials or private individuals.

Article V

The Contracting Parties undertake to enact, in accordance with their respective Constitutions, the necessary legislation to give effect to the provisions of the present Convention and, in particular, to provide effective penalties for persons guilty of genocide or any of the other acts enumerated in article III.

Article VI

Persons charged with genocide or any of the other acts enumerated in article III shall be tried by a competent tribunal of the State in the territory of which the act was committed, or by such international penal tribunal as may have jurisdiction with respect to those Contracting Parties which shall have accepted its jurisdiction.

Article VII

Genocide and the other acts enumerated in article III shall not be considered as political crimes for the purpose of extradition.

The Contracting Parties pledge themselves in such cases to grant extradition in accordance with their laws and treaties in force.

Article VIII

Any Contracting Party may call upon the competent organs of the United Nations to take such action under the Charter of the United Nations as they consider appropriate for the prevention and suppression of acts of genocide or any of the other acts enumerated in article III.

. . .

2. UNIVERSAL DECLARATION OF HUMAN RIGHTS[1]

Preamble

Whereas recognition of the inherent dignity and of the equal and in-

---

[1]Proclaimed by the General Assembly of the United Nations on 10 December 1948 in its resolution 217 (III), adopted by 48 votes to none, with eight abstentions.

alienable rights of all members of the human family is the foundation of freedom, justice and peace in the world,

Whereas disregard and contempt for human rights have resulted in barbarous acts which have outraged the conscience of mankind, and the advent of a world in which human beings shall enjoy freedom of speech and belief and freedom from fear and want has been proclaimed as the highest aspiration of the common people,

Whereas it is essential, if man is not to be compelled to have recourse, as a last resort, to rebellion against tyranny and oppression, that human rights should be protected by the rule of law,

Whereas it is essential to promote the development of friendly relations between nations,

Whereas the peoples of the United Nations have in the Charter reaffirmed their faith in fundamental human rights, in the dignity and worth of the human person and in the equal rights of men and women and have determined to promote social progress and better standards of life in larger freedom,

Whereas Member States have pledged themselves to achieve, in cooperation with the United Nations, the promotion of universal respect for and observance of human rights and fundamental freedoms,

Whereas a common understanding of these rights and freedoms is of the greatest importance for the full realization of this pledge,

Now, therefore,

The General Assembly

Proclaims this Universal Declaration of Human Rights as a common standard of achievement for all peoples and all nations, to the end that every individual and every organ of society, keeping this Declaration constantly in mind, shall strive by teaching and education to promote respect for these rights and freedoms and by progressive measures, national and international, to secure their universal and effective recognition and observance, both among the peoples of Member States themselves and among the peoples of territories under their jurisdiction.

Article 1

All human beings are born free and equal in dignity and rights. They are endowed with reason and conscience and should act towards one another in a spirit of brotherhood.

Article 2

Everyone is entitled to all the rights and freedoms set forth in this Declaration, without distinction of any kind, such as race, colour, sex, language, religion, political or other opinion, national or social origin, property, birth or other status.

Furthermore, no distinction shall be made on the basis of the political, jurisdictional or international status of the country or territory to which a person belongs, whether it be independent, trust, non-self-governing or under any other limitation of sovereignty.

Article 3

Everyone has the right to life, liberty and the security of person.

. . .

Article 6

Everyone has the right to recognition everywhere as a person before the law.

Article 7

All are equal before the law and are entitled without any discrimination to equal protection of the law. All are entitled to equal protection against any discrimination in violation of this Declaration and against any incitement to such discrimination.

Article 8

Everyone has the right to an effective remedy by the competent national tribunals for acts violating the fundamental rights granted him by the constitution or by law.

. . .

Article 12

No one shall be subjected to arbitrary interference with his privacy, family, home or correspondence, nor to attacks upon his honour and reputation. Everyone has the right to the protection of the law against such interference or attacks.

Article 13

1. Everyone has the right to freedom of movement and residence within the borders of each State.
2. Everyone has the right to leave any country, including his own, and to return to his country.

. . .

Article 16

1. Men and women of full age, without any limitation due to race, nationality or religion, have the right to marry and to found a family. They are entitled to equal rights as to marriage, during marriage and at its dissolution.

2. Marriage shall be entered into only with the free and full consent of the intending spouses.

3. The family is the natural and fundamental group unit of society and is entitled to protection by society and the State.

. . .

Article 18

Everyone has the right to freedom of thought, conscience and religion; this right includes freedom to change his religion or belief, and freedom, either alone or in community with others and in public or private, to manifest his religion or belief in teaching, practice, worship and observance.

Article 19

Everyone has the right to freedom of opinion and expression; this right includes freedom to hold opinions without interference and to seek, receive and impart information and ideas through any media and regardless of frontiers.

Article 22

Everyone, as a member of society, has the right to social security and is entitled to realization, through national effort and international cooperation and in accordance with the organization and resources of each State, of the economic, social and cultural rights indispensable for his dignity and the free development of his personality.

Article 23

1. Everyone has the right to work, to free choice of employment, to just and favourable conditions of work and to protection against unemployment.

2. Everyone, without any discrimination, has the right to equal pay for equal work.

3. Everyone who works has the right to just and favourable remuneration ensuring for himself and his family an existence worthy of human dignity, and supplemented, if necessary, by other means of social protection.

4. Everyone has the right to form and to join trade unions for the protection of his interests.

. . .

Article 25

1. Everyone has the right to a standard of living adequate for the health and well-being of himself and of his family, including food, clothing, housing and medical care and necessary social services, and the right

to security in the event of unemployment, sickness, disability, widow-hood, old age or other lack of livelihood in circumstances beyond his control.

2. Motherhood and childhood are entitled to special care and assistance. All children, whether born in or out of wedlock, shall enjoy the same social protection.

Article 26

1. Everyone has the right to education. Education shall be free, at least in the elementary and fundamental stages. Elementary education shall be compulsory. Technical and professional education shall be made generally available and higher education shall be equally accessible to all on the basis of merit.

2. Education shall be directed to the full development of the human personality and to the strengthening of respect for human rights and fundamental freedoms. It shall promote understanding, tolerance and friendship among all nations, racial or religious groups, and shall further the activities of the United Nations for the maintenance of peace.

3. Parents have a prior right to choose the kind of education that shall be given to their children.

Article 27

1. Everyone has the right freely to participate in the cultural life of the community, to enjoy the arts and to share in scientific advancement and its benefits.

. . .

Article 28

Everyone is entitled to a social and international order in which the rights and freedoms set forth in this Declaration can be fully realized.

Article 29

1. Everyone has duties to the community in which alone the free and full development of his personality is possible.

2. In the exercise of his rights and freedoms, everyone shall be subject only to such limitations as are determined by law solely for the purpose of securing due recognition and respect for the rights and freedoms of others and of meeting the just requirements of morality, public order and the general welfare in a democratic society.

3. These rights and freedoms may in no case be exercised contrary to the purposes and principles of the United Nations.

Article 30

Nothing in this Declaration may be interpreted as implying for any State, group or person any right to engage in any activity or to perform any act aimed at the destruction of any of the rights and freedoms set forth herein.

3. Convention Concerning Equal Remuneration for Men and Women Workers for Work of Equal Value[1]

The General Conference of the International Labour Organisation,
. . .

adopts this twenty-ninth day of June of the year one thousand nine hundred and fifty-one the following Convention, which may be cited as the Equal Remuneration Convention, 1951:

Article 1

For the purpose of this Convention:

(a) The term "remuneration" includes the ordinary, basic or minimum wage or salary and any additional emoluments whatsoever payable directly or indirectly, whether in cash or in kind, by the employer to the worker and arising out of the worker's employment;

(b) The term "equal remuneration for men and women workers for work of equal value" refers to rates of remuneration established without discrimination based on sex.

Article 2

1. Each Member shall, by means appropriate to the methods in operation for determining rates of remuneration, promote and, in so far as is consistent with such methods, ensure the application to all workers of the principle of equal remuneration for men and women workers for work of equal value.

2. This principle may be applied by means of:

(a) National laws or regulations;

(b) Legally established or recognized machinery for wage determination;

(c) Collective agreements between employers and workers; or

(d) A combination of these various means.

Article 3

1. Where such action will assist in giving effect to the provisions of this Convention, measures shall be taken to promote objective appraisal of jobs on the basis of the work to be performed.

---

[1]Adopted by 105 votes to 33, with 40 abstentions, 29 June 1951. Came into force: 23 May 1953.

2. The methods to be followed in this appraisal may be decided upon by the authorities responsible for the determination of rates of remuneration, or, where such rates are determined by collective agreements, by the parties thereto.

3. Differential rates between workers, which correspond, without regard to sex, to differences as determined by such objective appraisal, in the work to be performed shall not be considered as being contrary to the principle of equal remuneration for men and women workers for work of equal value.

Article 4

Each Member shall co-operate as appropriate with the employers' and workers' organizations concerned for the purpose of giving effect to the provisions of this Convention.

. . .

4. CONVENTION CONCERNING DISCRIMINATION IN RESPECT OF EMPLOYMENT AND OCCUPATION[1]

The General Conference of the International Labour Organisation,

. . .

adopts this twenty-fifth day of June of the year one thousand nine hundred and fifty-eight the following Convention, which may be cited as the Discrimination (Employment and Occupation) Convention, 1958:

1. For the purpose of this Convention the term "discrimination" includes:

(a) Any distinction, exclusion or preference made on the basis of race, colour, sex, religion, political opinion, national extraction or social origin, which has the effect of nullifying or impairing equality of opportunity or treatment in employment or occupation;

(b) Such other distinction, exclusion or preference which has the effect of nullifying or impairing equality opportunity or treatment in employment or occupation as may be determined by the Member concerned after consultation with representative employers' and workers' organizations, where such exist, and with other appropriate bodies.

2. Any distinction, exclusion or preference in respect of a particular job based on the inherent requirements thereof shall not be deemed to be discrimination.

3. For the purpose of this Convention the terms "employment" and "occupation" include access to vocational training, access to employ-

---

[1]Adopted 25 June 1958. Came into force 15 June 1960.

ment and to particular occupations, and terms and conditions of employment.

Article 2

Each Member for which this Convention is in force undertakes to declare and pursue a national policy designed to promote, by methods appropriate to national conditions and practice, equality of opportunity and treatment in respect of employment and occupation, with a view to eliminating any discrimination in respect thereof.

Article 3

Each Member for which this Convention is in force undertakes, by methods appropriate to national conditions and practice:

(a) To seek the co-operation of employers' and workers' organizations and other appropriate bodies in promoting the acceptance and observance of the policy;

(b) To enact such legislation and to promote such educational programmes as may be calculated to secure the acceptance and observance of the policy;

(c) To repeal any statutory provisions and modify any administrative instructions or practices which are inconsistent with the policy;

(d) To pursue the policy in respect of employment under the direct control of a national authority;

(e) To ensure observance of the policy in the activities of vocational guidance, vocational training and placement services under the direction of a national authority;

(f) To indicate in its annual reports on the application of the Convention the action taken in pursuance of the policy and the results secured by such action.

Article 4

Any measures affecting an individual who is justifiably suspected of, or engaged in, activities prejudicial to the security of the State shall not be deemed to be discrimination, provided that the individual concerned shall have the right to appeal to a competent body established in accordance with national practice.

Article 5

1. Special measures of protection or assistance provided in other Conventions or Recommendations adopted by the International Labour Conference shall not be deemed to be discrimination.

2. Any Member may, after consultation with representative employers' and workers' organizations, where such exist, determine that other special measures designed to meet the particular requirements of per-

sons who, for reasons such as sex, age disablement, family responsibilities or social or cultural status, are generally recognized to require special protection or assistance, shall not be deemed to be discrimination. . . .

5. DECLARATION OF THE RIGHTS OF THE CHILD[1]

Preamble

Whereas the peoples of the United Nations have, in the Charter, reaffirmed their faith in fundamental human rights and in the dignity and worth of the human person, and have determined to promote social progress and better standards of life in larger freedom,

Whereas the United Nations has, in the Universal Declaration of Human Rights, proclaimed that everyone is entitled to all the rights and freedoms set forth therein, without distinction of any kind, such as race, colour, sex, language, religion, political or other opinion, national or social origin, property, birth or other status,

Whereas the child, by reason of his physical and mental immaturity, needs special safeguards and care, including appropriate legal protection, before as well as after birth,

Whereas the need for such special safeguards has been stated in the Geneva Declaration of the Rights of the Child of 1924, and recognized in the Universal Declaration of Human Rights and in the statutes of specialized agencies and international organizations concerned with the welfare of children,

Whereas mankind owes to the child the best it has to give,

Now therefore,

The General Assembly

Proclaims this Declaration of the Rights of the Child to the end that he may have a happy childhood and enjoy for his own good and for the good of society the rights and freedoms herein set forth, and calls upon parents, upon men and women as individuals, and upon voluntary organizations, local authorities and national Governments to recognize these rights and strive for their observance by legislative and other measures progressively taken in accordance with the following principles:

Principle 1

The child shall enjoy all the rights set forth in this Declaration. Every child, without any exception whatsoever, shall be entitled to these rights, without distinction or discrimination on account of race, colour, sex, language, religion, political or other opinion, national or social origin, property, birth or other status, whether of himself or of his family.

---

[1]Proclaimed and adopted unanimously by the General Assembly of the United Nations on 20 November 1959 in its resolution 1386 XIV.

18

Principle 2

The child shall enjoy special protection, and shall be given opportunities and facilities, by law and by other means, to enable him to develop physically, mentally, morally, spiritually and socially in a healthy and normal manner and in conditions of freedom and dignity. In the enactment of laws for this purpose, the best interests of the child shall be the paramount consideration.

. . .

Principle 4

The child shall enjoy the benefits of social security. He shall be entitled to grow and develop in health; to this end, special care and protection shall be provided both to him and to his mother, including adequate pre-natal and post-natal care. The child shall have the right to adequate nutrition, housing, recreation and medical services.

. . .

Principle 6

The child, for the full and harmonious development of his personality, needs love and understanding. He shall, wherever possible, grow up in the care under the responsibility of his parents, and, in any case, in an atmosphere of affection and of moral and material security; a child of tender years shall not, save in exceptional circumstances, be separated from his mother. Society and the public authorities shall have the duty to extend particular care to children without a family and to those without adequate means of support. Payment of State and other assistance towards the maintenance of children of large families is desirable.

Principle 7

The child is entitled to receive education, which shall be free and compulsory, at least in the elementary stages. He shall be given an education which will promote his general culture, and enable him, on a basis of equal opportunity, to develop his abilities, his individual judgement, and his sense of moral and social responsibility, and to become a useful member of society.

The best interests of the child shall be the guiding principle of those responsible for his education and guidance; that responsibility lies in the first place with his parents.

The child shall have full opportunity for play and recreation, which should be directed to the same purposes as education; society and the public authorities shall endeavour to promote the enjoyment of this right.

Principle 8

The child shall in all circumstances be among the first to receive protection and relief.

Principle 9

The child shall be protected against all forms of neglect, cruelty and exploitation. He shall not be the subject of traffic, in any form.

The child shall not be admitted to employment before an appropriate minimum age; he shall in no case be caused or permitted to engage in any occupation or employment which would prejudice his health or education, or interfere with his physical, mental or moral development.

. . .

6. CONVENTION AGAINST DISCRIMINATION IN EDUCATION[1]

The General Conference of the United Nations Educational, Scientific and Cultural Organization, . . .

Recalling that the Universal Declaration of Human Rights asserts the principle of non-discrimination and proclaims that every person has the right to education,

Considering that discrimination in education is a violation of rights enunciated in that Declaration,

Considering that, under the terms of its Constitution, the United Nations Educational, Scientific and Cultural Organization has the purpose of instituting collaboration among the nations with a view to furthering for all universal respect for human rights and equality of educational opportunity,

Recognizing that, consequently, the United Nations Educational, Scientific and Cultural Organization, while respecting the diversity of national educational systems, has the duty not only to proscribe any form of discrimination in education but also to promote equality of opportunity and treatment for all in education,

. . .

Adopts this Convention on the fourteenth day of December 1960.

Article 1

1. For the purposes of this Convention, the term "discrimination" includes any distinction, exclusion, limitation or preference which, being based on race, colour, sex, language, religion, political or other opinion, national or social origin, economic condition or birth, has the purpose or

---

[1]Adopted by 60 votes to none, with 2 abstentions, 14 December 1960. Came into force 22 May 1962.

effect of nullifying or impairing equality of treatment in education and in particular:

(a) Of depriving any person or group of persons of access to education of any type or at any level;

(b) Of limiting any person or group of persons to education of an inferior standard;

(c) Subject to the provisions of article 2 of this Convention, of establishing or maintaining separate educational systems or institutions for persons or groups of persons; or

(d) Of inflicting on any person or group of persons conditions which are incompatible with the dignity of man.

2. For the purposes of this Convention, the term "education" refers to all types and levels of education, and includes access to education, the standard and quality of education, and the conditions under which it is given.

Article 2

When permitted in a State, the following situations shall not be deemed to constitute discrimination, within the meaning of article 1 of this Convention:

(a) The establishment or maintenance of separate educational systems or institutions for pupils of the two sexes, if these systems or institutions offer equivalent access to education, provide a teaching staff with qualifications of the same standard as well as school premises and equipment of the same quality, and afford the opportunity to take the same or equivalent courses of study;

(b) The establishment or maintenance, for religious or linguistic reasons, of separate educational systems or institutions offering an education which is in keeping with the wishes of the pupil's parents or legal guardians, if participation in such systems or attendance at such institutions is optional and if the education provided conforms to such standards as may be laid down or approved by the competent authorities, in particular for education of the same level;

(c) The establishment or maintenance of private educational institutions, if the object of the institutions is not to secure the exclusion of any group but to provide educational facilities in addition to those provided by the public authorities, if the institutions are conducted in accordance with that object, and if the education provided conforms with such standards as may be laid down or approved by the competent authorities, in particular for education of the same level.

Article 3

In order to eliminate and prevent discrimination within the meaning of this Convention, the States Parties thereto undertake:

(a) To abrogate any statutory provisions and any administrative instructions and to discontinue any administrative practices which involve discrimination in education;

(b) To ensure, by legislation where necessary, that there is no discrimination in the admission of pupils to educational institutions;

(c) Not to allow any differences of treatment by the public authorities between nationals, except on the basis of merit or need, in the matter of school fees and the grant of scholarships or other forms of assistance to pupils and necessary permits and facilities for the pursuit of studies in foreign countries;

(d) Not to allow, in any form of assistance granted by the public authorities to educational institutions, any restrictions or preference based solely on the ground that pupils belong to a particular group;

(e) To give foreign nationals resident within their territory the same access to education as that given to their own nationals.

Article 4

The States Parties to this Convention undertake furthermore to formulate, develop and apply a national policy which, by methods appropriate to the circumstances and to national usage, will tend to promote equality of opportunity and of treatment in the matter of education and in particular:

(a) To make primary education free and compulsory; make secondary education in its different forms generally available and accessible to all; make higher education equally accessible to all on the basis of individual capacity; assure compliance by all with the obligation to attend school prescribed by law;

(b) To ensure that the standards of education are equivalent in all public education institutions of the same level, and that the conditions relating to the quality of the education provided are also equivalent;

(c) To encourage and intensify by appropriate methods the education of persons who have not received any primary education or who have not completed the entire primary education course and the continuation of their education on the basis of individual capacity;

(d) To provide training for the teaching profession without discrimination.

Article 5

1. The States Parties to this Convention agree that:

(a) Education shall be directed to the full development of the human personality and to the strengthening of respect for human rights and fundamental freedoms; it shall promote understanding, tolerance and friendship among all nations, racial or religious groups, and shall further the activities of the United Nations for the maintenance fo peace;

(b) It is essential to respect the liberty of parents and, where applicable, of legal guardians, firstly to choose for their children institutions other than those maintained by the public authorities but conforming to such minimum educational standards as may be laid down or approved by the competent authorities and, secondly, to ensure in a manner consistent with the procedures followed in the State for the application of its legislation, the religious and moral education of the children in conformity with their own convictions; and no person or group of persons should be compelled to receive religious instruction inconsistent with his or their conviction;

(c) It is essential to recognize the right of members of national minorities to carry on their own educational activities, including the maintenance of schools and, depending on the educational policy of each State, the use or the teaching of their own language, provided however:

(i) That this right is not exercised in a manner which prevents the members of these minorities from understanding the culture and language of the community as a whole and from participating its activities, or which prejudices national sovereignty;

(ii) That the standard of education is not lower than the general standard laid down or approved by the competent authorities; and

(iii) That attendance at such schools is optional.

2. The States Parties to this Convention undertake to take all necessary measures to ensure the application of the principles enuniciated in paragraph 1 of this article.

. . .

7. CONVENTION CONCERNING BASIC AIMS AND STANDARDS OF SOCIAL POLICY[1]

The General Conference of the International Labour Organisation,

. . .

Considering that economic development must serve as a basis for social progress, and

Considering that every effort should be made, on an international, regional or national basis, to secure financial and technical assistance safeguarding the interests of the population, and

Considering that, in appropriate cases, international, regional or national action should be taken with a view to establishing conditions of trade which would encourage production at a high level of efficiency and make possible the maintenance of a reasonable standard of living, and

Considering that all possible steps should be taken by appropriate international, regional and national measures to promote improvement in

---

[1]Adopted by 294 votes to none with 15 abstentions. Came into force 23 April 1964.

such fields as public health, housing, nutrition, education, the welfare of children, the status of women, conditions of employment, the remuneration of wage earners and independent producers, the protection of migrant workers, social security, standards of public services and general production, and

Considering that all possible steps should be taken effectively to interest and associate the population in the framing and execution of measures of social progress,

Adopts this twenty-second day of June of the year one thousand nine hundred and sixty-two the following Convention, which may be cited as the Social Policy (Basic Aims and Standards) Convention, 1962:

PART I. GENERAL PRINCIPLES

Article 1

1. All policies shall be primarily directed to the well-being and development of the population and to the promotion of its desire for social progress.

2. All policies of more general application shall be formulated with due regard to their effect upon the well-being of the population.

PART II. IMPROVEMENT OF STANDARDS OF LIVING

Article 2

The improvement of standards of living shall be regarded as the principal objective in the planning of economic development.

Article 3

1. All practicable measures shall be taken in the planning of economic development to harmonize such development with the healthy evolution of the communities concerned.

2. In particular, efforts shall be made to avoid the disruption of family life and of traditional social units, especially by—

(a) close study of the causes and effect of migratory movements and appropriate action where necessary;

(b) the promotion of town and village planning in areas where economic needs result in the concentration of population;

(c) the prevention and elimination of congestion in urban areas;

(d) the improvement of living conditions in rural areas and the establishment of suitable industries in rural areas where adequate manpower is available.

Article 5

1. Measures shall be taken to secure for independent producers and wage earners conditions which will give them scope to improve living standards by their own efforts and will ensure the maintenance of minimum standards of living as ascertained by means of official inquiries into living conditions, conducted after consultation with the representative organizations of employers and workers.

2. In ascertaining the minimum standards of living, account shall be taken of such essential family needs of the workers as food and its nutritive value, housing, clothing, medical care and education.

PART III. PROVISIONS CONCERNING MIGRANT WORKERS

Article 6

Where the circumstances under which workers are employed involve their living away from their homes, the terms and conditions of their employment shall take account of their normal family needs.

. . .

PART VI. EDUCATION AND TRAINING

Article 15

1. Adequate provision shall be made to the maximum extent possible under local conditions, for the progressive development of broad systems of education, vocational training and apprenticeship, with a view to the effective preparation of children and young persons of both sexes for a useful occupation.

2. National laws or regulations shall prescribe the school-leaving age and the minimum age for and conditions of employment.

3. In order that the child population may be able to profit by existing facilities for education and in order that the extension of such facilities may not be hindered by a demand for child labour, the employment of persons below the school-leaving age during the hours when the schools are in session shall be prohibited in areas where educational facilities are provided on a scale adequate for the majority of the children of school age.

8. CONVENTION ON CONSENT TO MARRIAGE, MINIMUM AGE FOR MARRIAGE AND REGISTRATION OF MARRIAGES[1]

---

[1]Opened for signature and ratification by General Assembly resolution 1763 A (XVII) of 7 November 1962. Adopted by 92 votes to none, with 7 abstentions. Came into force 9 December 1964.

The Contracting States,

Desiring, in conformity with the Charter of the United Nations, to promote universal respect for, and observance of, human rights and fundamental freedoms for all, without distinction as to race, sex, language or religion,

. . .

Recalling further that the General Assembly of the United Nations declared, by resolution 843 (IX) of 17 December 1954, that certain customs, ancient laws and practices relating to marriage and the family were inconsistent with the principles set forth in the Charter of the United Nations and in the Universal Declaration of Human Rights,

Reaffirming that all States, including those which have or assume responsibility for the administration of Non-Self-Governing and Trust Territories until their achievement of independence, should take all appropriate measures with a view to abolishing such customs, ancient laws and practices by ensuring, *inter alia,* complete freedom in the choice of a spouse, eliminating completely child marriages and the betrothal of young girls before the age of puberty, establishing appropriate penalties where necessary and establishing a civil or other register in which all marriages will be recorded,

Hereby agree as hereinafter provided:

Article 1

1. No marriage shall be legally entered into without the full and free consent of both parties, such consent to be expressed by them in person after due publicity and in the presence of the authority competent to solemnize the marriage and of witnesses, as prescribed by law.

2. Notwithstanding anything in paragraph 1 above, it shall not be necessary for one of the parties to be present when the competent authority is satisfied that the circumstances are exceptional and that the party has, before a competent authority and in such manner as may be prescribed by law, expressed and not withdrawn consent.

Article 2

States parties to the present Convention shall take legislative action to specify a minimum age for marriage. No marriage shall be legally entered into by any person under this age, except where a competent authority has granted a dispensation as to age, for serious reasons, in the interest of the intending spouses.

Article 3

All marriages shall be registered in an appropriate official register by the competent authority.

. . .

9. UNITED NATIONS DECLARATION ON THE ELIMINATION OF ALL FORMS OF RACIAL DISCRIMINATION[1]

The General Assembly,

Considering that the Charter of the United Nations is based on the principles of the dignity and equality of all human beings and seeks, among other basic objectives, to achieve international co-operation in promoting and encouraging respect for human rights and fundamental freedoms for all without distinction as to race, sex, language or religion,

Considering that the Universal Declaration of Human Rights proclaims that all human beings are born free and equal in dignity and rights and that everyone is entitled to all the rights and freedoms set out in the Declaration, without distinction of any kind, in particular as to race, colour or national origin,

Considering that the Universal Declaration of Human Rights proclaims further that all are equal before the law and are entitled without any discrimination to equal protection of the law and that all are entitled to equal protection against any discrimination and against any incitement to such discrimination,

Considering, that the United Nations has condemned colonialism and all practices of segregation and discrimination associated therewith, and that the Declaration on the granting of independence to colonial countries and peoples proclaims in particular the necessity of bringing colonialism to a speedy and unconditional end,

Considering that any doctrine of racial differentiation or superiority is scientifically false, morally condemnable, socially unjust and dangerous, and that there is no justification for racial discrimination either in theory or in practice,

Taking into account the other resolutions adopted by the General Assembly and the international instruments adopted by the specialized agencies, in particular the International Labour Organisation and the United Nations Educational, Scientific and Cultural Organization, in the field of discrimination,

Taking into account the fact that, although international action and efforts in a number of countries have made it possible to achieve progress in that field, discrimination based on race, colour or ethnic origin in certain areas of the world continues none the less to give cause for serious concern,

Alarmed by the manifestations of racial discrimination still in evidence in some areas of the world, some of which are imposed by certain Governments by means of legislative, administrative or other measures, in

---

[1] Proclaimed by the General Assembly of the United Nations on 20 November 1963 (resolution 1904 (XVIII)). Adopted unanimously.

the form, *inter alia,* of *apartheid,* segregation and separation, as well as by the promotion and dissemination of doctrines of racial superiority and expansionism in certain areas,

Convinced that all forms of racial discrimination and, still more so, governmental policies based on the prejudice of racial superiority or on racial hatred, besides constituting a violation of fundamental human rights, tend to jeopardize friendly relations among peoples, co-operation between nations and international peace and security,

Convinced also that racial discrimination harms not only those who are its objects but also those who practise it,

Convinced further that the building of a world society free from all forms of racial segregation and discrimination, factors which create hatred and division among men, is one of the fundamental objectives of the United Nations,

1. *Solemnly affirms* the necessity of speedily eliminating racial discrimination throughout the world, in all its forms and manifestations, and of securing understandings of and respect for the dignity of the human person;

2. *Solemnly affirms* the necessity of adopting national and international measures to that end, including teaching, education and information, in order to secure the universal and effective recognition and observance of the principles set forth below;

3. *Proclaims* this Declaration:

Article 1

Discrimination between human beings on the ground of race, colour or ethnic origin is an offence to human dignity and shall be condemned as a denial of the principles of the Charter of the United Nations, as a violation of the human rights and fundamental freedoms proclaimed in the Universal Declaration of Human Rights, as an obstacle to friendly and peaceful relations among nations and as a fact capable of disturbing peace and security among peoples.

Article 2

1. No State, institution, group or individual shall make any discrimination whatsoever in matters of human rights and fundamental freedoms in the treatment of persons, groups of persons or institutions on the ground of race, colour or ethnic origin.

2. No State shall encourage, advocate or lend its support, through police action or otherwise, to any discrimination based on race, colour, or ethnic origin by any group, institution or individual.

3. Special concrete measures shall be taken in appropriate circumstances in order to secure adequate development or protection of individuals belonging to certain racial groups with the object of ensuring the full

enjoyment by such individuals of human rights and fundamental freedoms. These measures shall in no circumstances have as a consequence the maintenance of unequal or separate rights for different racial groups.

Article 3

1. Particular efforts shall be made to prevent discrimination based on race, colour, or ethnic origin, especially in the fields of civil rights, access to citizenship, education, religion, employment, occupation and housing.

2. Everyone shall have equal access to any place or facility intended for use by the general public, without distinction as to race, colour or ethnic origin.

Article 4

All States shall take effective measures to revise governmental and other public policies and to rescind laws and regulations which have the effect of creating and perpetuating racial discrimination wherever it still exists. They should pass legislation for prohibiting such discrimination and should take all appropriate measures to combat those prejudices which lead to racial discrimination.

Article 5

An end shall be put without delay to governmental and other public policies of racial segregation and especially policies of *apartheid,* as well as all forms of racial discrimination and separation resulting from such policies.

Article 6

No discrimination by reason of race, colour or ethnic origin shall be admitted in the enjoyment by any person of political and citizenship rights in his country, in particular the right to participate in elections through universal and equal suffrage and to take part in the Government. Everyone has the right of equal access to public service in his country.

Article 7

1. Everyone has the right to equality before the law and to equal justice under the law. Everyone, without distinction as to race, colour or ethnic origin, has the right to security of person and protection by the State against violence or bodily harm, whether inflicted by government officials or by any individual group or institution.

2. Everyone shall have the right to an effective remedy and protection against any discrimination he may suffer on the ground of race, colour or ethnic origin with respect to his fundamental rights and freedoms through independent national tribunals competent to deal with such matters.

Article 8

All effective steps shall be taken immediately in the fields of teaching, education and information, with a view to eliminating racial discrimination and prejudice and promoting understanding, tolerance and friendship among nations and racial groups, as well as to propagating the purposes and principles of the Charter of the United Nations, of the Universal Declaration of Human Rights, and of the Declaration on the Granting of Independence to Colonial Countries and Peoples.

Article 9

1. All propaganda and organizations based on ideas or theories of the superiority of one race or group of persons of one colour or ethnic origin with a view to justifying or promoting racial discrimination in any form shall be severely condemned.

2. All incitement to or acts of violence, whether by individuals or organizations against any race or group of persons of another colour or ethnic origin shall be considered an offence against society and punishable under law.

3. In order to put into effect the purposes and principles of the present Declaration, all States shall take immediate and positive measures, including legislative and other measures, to prosecute and/or outlaw organizations which promote or incite to racial discrimination, or incite to or use violence for purposes or discrimination based on race, colour or ethnic origin.

Article 10

The United Nations, the specialized agencies, States and non-governmental organizations shall do all in their power to promote energetic action which, by combining legal and other practical measures, will make possible the abolition of all forms of racial discrimination. They shall, in particular, study the causes of such discrimination with a view to recommending appropriate and effective measures to combat and eliminate it.

Article 11

Every State shall promote respect for and observance of human rights and fundamental freedoms in accordance with the Charter of the United Nations and shall fully and faithfully observe the provisions of the present Declaration, the Universal Declaration of Human Rights and the Declaration on the Granting of Independence to Colonial Countries and Peoples.

10. Convention Concerning Employment Policy[1]

The General Conference of the International Labour Organisation,
. . .

adopts this ninth day of July of the year one thousand nine hundred and sixty-four the following Convention, which may be cited as the Employment Policy Convention, 1964:

Article 1

1. With a view to stimulating economic growth and development, raising levels of living, meeting manpower requirements and overcoming unemployment and under-employment, each Member shall declare and pursue, as a major goal, an active policy designed to promote full, productive and freely chosen employment.

2. The said policy shall aim at ensuring that:

(a) There is work for all who are available for and seeking work;

(b) Such work is as productive as possible;

(c) There is freedom of choice of employment and the fullest possible opportunity for each worker to qualify for, and to use his skills and endowments in, a job for which he is well suited, irrespective of race, colour, sex, religion, political opinion, national extraction or social origin.

3. The said policy shall take due account of the stage and level of economic development and the mutual relationships between employment objectives and other economic and social objectives, and shall be pursued by methods that are appropriate to national conditions and practices.

Article 2

Each Member shall, by such methods and to such extent as may be appropriate under national conditions:

(a) Decide on and keep under review, within the framework of a coordinated economic and social policy, the measures to be adopted for attaining the objectives specified in article 1;

(b) Take such steps as may be needed, including when appropriate the establishment of programmes, for the application of the measures.

Article 3

In the application of this Convention, representatives of the persons affected by the measures to be taken, and in particular representatives of employers and workers, shall be consulted concerning employment policies, with a view to taking fully into account their experience and views and securing their full co-operation in formulating and enlisting support for such policies.

. . .

---

[1]Adopted by 170 votes to 44, with 40 abstentions. Came into force 15 July 1966.

11. International Convention on the Elimination of All Forms of Racial Discrimination[1]

The States Parties to this Convention,

Considering that the Charter of the United Nations is based on the principles of the dignity and equality inherent in all human beings, and that all Member States pledged themselves to take joint and separate action, in co-operation with the Organization, for the achievement of one of the purposes of the United Nations which is to promote and encourage universal respect for and observance of human rights and fundamental freedoms for all, without distinction as to race, sex, language or religion,

Considering that the Universal Declaration of Human Rights proclaims that all human beings are born free and equal in dignity and rights and that everyone is entitled to all the rights and freedoms set out therein, without distinction of any kind, in particular as to race, colour or national origin,

Considering that all human beings are equal before the law and are entitled to equal protection of the law against any discrimination and against any incitement to discrimination,

Considering that the United Nations has condemned colonialism and all practices of segregation and discrimination associated therewith, in whatever form and wherever they exist, and that the Declaration on the Granting of Independence to Colonial Countries and Peoples of 14 December 1960 (General Assembly resolution 1514 (XV)) has affirmed and solemnly proclaimed the necessity of bringing them to a speedy and unconditional end,

Considering that the United Nations Declaration on the Elimination of All Forms of Racial Discrimination of 20 November 1963 (General Assembly resolution 1904 (XVIII)) solemnly affirms the necessity of speedily eliminating racial discrimination throughout the world in all its forms and manifestations and of securing understanding of and respect for the dignity of the human person,

Convinced that any doctrine of superiority based on racial differentiation is scientifically false, morally condemnable, socially unjust and dangerous, and that there is no justification for racial discrimination, in theory or in practice, anywhere,

Reaffirming that discrimination between human beings on the grounds of race, colour or ethnic origin is an obstacle to friendly and peaceful relations among nations and is capable of disturbing peace and security among peoples and the harmony of persons living side by side even within one and the same State,

---

[1]Adopted unanimously and opened for signature and ratification by General Assembly resolution 2106 A (XX) of 21 December 1965. Had not come into force on 1 July 1973.

Convinced that the existence of racial barriers is repugnant to the ideals of any human society,

Alarmed by manifestations of racial discrimination still in evidence in some areas of the world and by governmental policies based on racial superiority or hatred, such as policies of *apartheid,* segregation or separation,

Resolved to adopt all necessary measures for speedily eliminating racial discrimination in all its forms and manifestations, and to prevent and combat racist doctrines and practices in order to promote understanding between races and to build an international community free from all forms of racial segregation and racial discrimination,

Bearing in mind the Convention concerning Discrimination in respect of Employment and Occupation adopted by the International Labour Organisation in 1958, and the Convention against Discrimination in Education adopted by the United Nations Educational, Scientific and Cultural Organization in 1960,

Desiring to implement the principles embodied in the United Nations Declaration on the Elimination of All Forms of Racial Discrimination and to secure the earliest adoption of practical measures to that end,

Have agreed as follows:

Article 1

1. In this Convention, the term "racial discrimination" shall mean any distinction, exclusion, restriction or preference based on race, colour, descent, or national or ethnic origin which has the purpose or effect of nullifying or impairing the recognition, enjoyment or exercise, on an equal footing, of human rights and fundamental freedoms in the political, economic, social, cultural or any other field of public life.

2. This Convention shall not apply to distinctions, exclusions, restrictions or preferences made by a State Party to this Convention between citizens and non-citizens.

3. Nothing in this Convention may be interpreted as affecting in any way the legal provisions of States Parties concerning nationality, citizenship or naturalization, provided that such provisions do not discriminate against any particular nationality.

4. Special measures taken for the sole purpose of securing adequate advancement of certain racial or ethnic groups or individuals requiring such protection as may be necessary in order to ensure such groups or individuals equal enjoyment or exercise of human rights and fundamental freedoms shall not be deemed racial discrimination, provided, however, that such measures do not, as consequence, lead to the maintenance of separate rights for different racial groups and that they shall not be continued after the objectives for which they were taken have been achieved.

Article 2

1. States Parties condemn racial discrimination and undertake to pursue by all appropriate means and without delay a policy of eliminating racial discrimination in all its forms and promoting understanding among all races, and, to this end:

(a) Each State Party undertakes to engage in no act or practice of racial discrimination against persons, groups of persons or institutions and to ensure that all public authorities and public institutions, national and local, shall act in conformity with this obligation;

(b) Each State Party undertakes not to sponsor, defend or support racial discrimination by any persons or organizations;

(c) Each State Party shall take effective measures to review governmental, national and local policies, and to amend, rescind or nullify any laws and regulations which have the effect of creating or perpetuating racial discrimination wherever it exists;

(d) Each State Party shall prohibit and bring to an end, by all appropriate means, including legislation as required by circumstances, racial discrimination by any persons, group or organization;

(e) Each State Party undertakes to encourage, where appropriate, integrationist multi-racial organizations and movements and other means of eliminating barriers between races, and to discourage anything which tends to strengthen racial division.

2. States Parties shall, when the circumstances so warrant, take, in the social, economic, cultural and other fields, special and concrete measures to ensure the adequate development and protection of certain racial groups or individuals belonging to them, for the purpose of guaranteeing them the full and equal enjoyment of human rights and fundamental freedoms. These measures shall in no case entail as a consequence the maintenance of unequal or separate rights for different racial groups after the objectives for which they were taken have been achieved.

Article 3

States Parties particularly condemn racial segregation and *apartheid* and undertake to prevent, prohibit and eradicate all practices of this nature in territories under their jurisdiction.

Article 4

States Parties condemn all propaganda and all organizations which are based on ideas or theories of superiority of one race or group of persons of one colour or ethnic origin, or which attempt to justify or promote racial hatred and discrimination in any form, and undertake to adopt immediate and positive measures designed to eradicate all incitement to, or acts of, such discrimination and, to this end, with due regard to the principles embodied in the Universal Declaration of Human Rights and the rights expressly set forth in article 5 of this Convention, *inter alia:*

(a) Shall declare an offence punishable by law all dissemination of ideas based on racial superiority or hatred, incitement to racial discrimination, as well as all acts of violence or incitement to such acts against any race or group of persons of another colour or ethnic origin, and also the provision of any assistance to racist activities, including the financing thereof;

(b) Shall declare illegal and prohibit organizations, and also organized and all other propaganda activities, which promote and incite racial discrimination, and shall recognize participation in such organization or activities as an offence punishable by law;

(c) Shall not permit public authorities or public institutions, national or local, to promote or incite racial discrimination.

Article 5

In compliance with the fundamental obligations laid down in article 2 of this Convention, States Parties undertake to prohibit and to eliminate racial discrimination in all its forms and to guarantee the right of everyone, without distinction as to race, colour, or national or ethnic origin, to equality before the law, notably in the enjoyment of the following rights:

(a) The right to equal treatment before the tribunals and all other organs administering justice;

(b) The right to security of person and protection by the State against violence or bodily harm, whether inflicted by government officials or by any individual, group or institution;

(c) Political rights, in particular the rights to participate in elections — to vote and to stand for election — on the basis of universal and equal suffrage, to take part in the Government as well as in the conduct of public affairs at any level and to have equal access to public service;

(d) Other civil rights, in particular:

(i) The right to freedom of movement and residence within the border of the State;

(ii) The right to leave any country, including one's own, and to return to one's country;

(iii) The right to nationality;

(iv) The right to marriage and choice of spouse;

(v) The right to own property alone as well as in association with others;

(vi) The right to inherit;

(vii) The right to freedom of thought, conscience and religion;

(viii) The right to freedom of opinion and expression;

(ix) The right to freedom of peaceful assembly and association;

(e) Economic, social and cultural rights, in particular:

(i) The rights to work, to free choice of employment, to just and favourable conditions of work, to protection against unemployment, to equal pay for equal work, to just and favourable remuneration;

(ii) The right to form and join trade unions;

(iii) The right to housing;

(iv) The right to public health, medical care, social security and social services;

(v) The right to education and training;

(vi) The right to equal participation in cultural activities;

(f) The right of access to any place or service intended for use by the general public, such as transport, hotels, restaurants, cafés, theatres and parks.

Article 6

States Parties shall assure to everyone within their jurisdiction effective protection and remedies, through the competent national tribunals and other State institutions, against any acts of racial discrimination which violate his human rights and fundamental freedoms contrary to this Convention, as well as the right to seek from such tribunals just and adequate reparation or satisfaction for any damage suffered as a result of such discrimination.

Article 7

States Parties undertake to adopt immediate and effective measures, particularly in the fields of teaching, education, culture and information, with a view to combating prejudices which lead to racial discrimination and to promoting understanding, tolerance and friendship among nations and racial or ethnical groups, as well as to propagating the purposes and principles of the Charter of the United Nations, the Universal Declaration of Human Rights, the United Nations Declaration on the Elimination of All Forms of Racial Discrimination, and this Convention.

12. International Covenant on Economic, Social and Cultural Rights[1]

Preamble

The States Parties to the Present Covenant,

Considering that, in accordance with the principles proclaimed in the Charter of the United Nations, recognition of the inherent dignity and of the equal and inalienable rights of all members of the human family is the foundation of freedom, justice and peace in the world,

Recognizing that these rights derive from the inherent dignity of the human person,

Recognizing that, in accordance with the Universal Declaration of Human Rights, the ideal of free human beings enjoying freedom from fear and want can only be achieved if conditions are created whereby everyone may enjoy his economic, social and cultural rights, as well as his civil and political rights,

Considering the obligation of States under the Charter of the United Nations to promote universal respect for, and observance of, human rights and freedoms,

Realizing that the individual, having duties to other individuals and to the community to which he belongs, is under a responsibility, to strive for the promotion and observance of the rights recognized in the present Covenant,

Agree upon the following articles:

. . .

Article 2

1. Each State Party to the present Covenant undertakes to take steps, individually and through international assistance and co-operation, especially economic and technical, to the maximum of its available resources, with a veiw to achieving progressively the full realization of the rights recognized in the present Covenant by all appropriate means, including particularly the adoption of legislative measures.

2. The States Parties to the present Covenant undertake to guarantee that the rights enunciated in the present Covenant will be exercised without discrimination of any kind as to race, colour, sex, language, religion, political or other opinion, national or social origin, property, birth or other status.

. . .

---

[1]Adopted by 105 votes to none, with no abstentions and opened for signature, ratification and accession by General Assembly resolution 2200 A (XXI) of 16 December 1966. Had not come into force on 1 July 1973.

Article 3

The States Parties to the present Covenant undertake to ensure the equal right of men and women to the enjoyment of all economic, social and cultural rights set forth in the present Covenant.

Article 4

The States Parties to the present Covenant recognize that, in the enjoyment of those rights provided by the State in conformity with the present Covenant, the State may subject such rights only to such limitations as are determined by law only in so far as this may be compatible with the nature of these rights and solely for the purpose of promoting the general welfare in a democratic society.

Article 5

1. Nothing in the present Covenant may be interpreted as implying for any State, group or person any right to engage in any activity or to perform any act aimed at the destruction of any of the rights or freedoms recognized herein, or at their limitation to a greater extent than is provided for in the present Covenant.

2. No restriction upon or derogation from any of the fundamental human rights recognized or existing in any country in virtue of law, conventions, regulations or custom shall be admitted on the pretext that the present Covenant does not recognize such rights or that it recognizes them to a lesser extent.

Article 6

1. The States Parties to the present Covenant recognize the right to work, which includes the right of everyone to the opportunity to gain his living by work which he freely chooses or accepts, and will take appropriate steps to safeguard this right.

2. The steps to be taken by a State Party to the present Covenant to achieve the full realization of this right shall include technical and vocational guidance and training programmes, policies and techniques to achieve steady economic, social and cultural development and full and productice employment under conditions safeguarding fundamental political and economic freedoms to the individual.

Article 7

The States Parties to the present Covenant recognize the right of everyone to the enjoyment of just and favourable conditions of work which ensure, in particular:

(a) Remuneration which provides all workers, as a minimum, with:

(i) Fair wages and equal remuneration for work of equal value without distinction of any kind, in particular women being guaranteed condition of work not inferior to those enjoyed by men, with equal pay for equal work;

(ii) A decent living for themselves and their families in accordance with the provisions of the present Covenant;

(b) Safe and healthy working conditions;

(c) Equal opportunity for everyone to be promoted in his employment to an appropriate higher level, subject to no considerations other than those of seniority and competence;

(d) Rest, leisure and reasonable limitation of working hours and periodic holidays with pay, as well as remuneration for public holidays.

. . .

Article 9

The States Parties to the present Covenant recognize the right of everyone to social security, including social insurance.

Article 10

The States Parties to the present Convenant recognize that:

1. The widest possible protection and assistance should be accorded to the family, which is the natural and fundamental group unit of society, particularly for its establishment and while it is responsible for the care and education of dependent children. Marriage must be entered into with the free consent of the intending spouses.

2. Special protection should be accorded to mothers during a reasonable period before and after childbirth. During such period working mothers should be accorded paid leave or leave with adequate social security benefits.

3. Special measures of protection and assistance should be taken on behalf of all children and young persons without any discrimination for reasons of parentage or other conditions. Children and young persons should be protected from economic and social exploitation. Their employment in work harmful to their morals or health or dangerous to life or likely to hamper their normal development should be punishable by law. States should also set age limits below which the paid employment of child labour should be prohibited and punishable by law.

Article 11

1. The States Parties to the present Covenant recognize the right of everyone to an adequate standard of living for himself and his family, including adequate food, clothing and housing, and to the continuous im-

provement of living conditions. The States Parties will take appropriate steps to ensure the realization of this right, recognizing to this effect the essential importance of international co-operation based on free consent.

2. The States Parties of the present Covenant, recognizing the fundamental right of everyone to be free from hunger, shall take, individually and through international co-operation, the measures, including specific programmes, which are needed:

(a) To improve methods of production, conservation and distribution of food by making full use of technical and scientific knowledge, by disseminating knowledge of the principles of nutrition and by developing or reforming agrarian systems in such a way as to achieve the most efficient development and utilization of natural resources;

(b) Taking into account the problems of both food-importing and food-exporting countries, to ensure an equitable distribution of world food supplies in relation to need.

Article 12

1. The States Parties to the present Covenant recognize the right of everyone to the enjoyment of the highest attainable standard of physical and mental health.

2. The steps to be taken by the States Parties to the present Covenant to achieve the full realization of this right shall include those necessary for:

(a) The provision for the reduction of the stillbirth-rate and of infant mortality and for the healthy development of the child;

(b) The improvement of all aspects of environmental and industrial hygiene;

(c) The prevention, treatment and control of epidemic, endemic, occupational and other diseases;

(d) The creation of conditions which would assure to all medical service and medical attention in the event of sickness.

Article 13

1. The States Parties to the present Covenant recognize the right of everyone to education. They agree that education shall be directed to the full development of the human personality and the sense of its dignity, and shall strengthen the respect for human rights and fundamental freedoms. They further agree that education shall enable all persons to participate effectively in a free society, promote understanding, tolerance and friendship among all nations and all racial, ethnic or religious groups, and further the activities of the United Nations for the maintenance of peace.

2. The States Parties to the present Covenant recognize that, with a view to achieving the full realization of this right:

(a) Primary education shall be compulsory and available free to all;

(b) Secondary education in its different forms, including technical and vocational secondary education, shall be made generally available and accessible to all by every appropriate means, and in particular by the progressive introduction of free education;

(c) Higher education shall be made equally accessible to all, on the basis of capacity, by every appropriate means, and in particular by the progressive introduction of free education;

(d) Fundamental education shall be encouraged or intensified as far as possible for those persons who have not received or completed the whole period of their primary education;

(e) The development of a system of schools at all levels shall be actively pursued, an adequate fellowship system shall be established, and the material conditions of teaching staff shall be continuously improved.

3. The States Parties to the present Covenant undertake to have respect for the liberty of parents and, when applicable, legal guardians to choose for their children schools, other than those established by the public authorities, which conform to such minimum educational standards as may be laid down or approved by the State and to ensure the religious and moral education of their children in conformity with their own convictions.

4. No part of this article shall be construed so as to interfere with the liberty of individuals and bodies to establish and direct educational institutions, subject always to the observance of the principles set forth in paragraph 1 of this article and to the requirement that the education given in such institutions shall conform to such minimum standards as may be laid down by the State.

Article 14

Each State Party to the present Covenant which, at the time of becoming a Party, has not been able to secure in its metropolitan territory or other territories under its jurisdiction compulsory primary education, free of charge, undertakes, within two years, to work out and adopt a detailed plan of action for the progressive implementation, within a reasonable number of years, to be fixed in the plan, of the principle of compulsory education free of charge for all.

Article 15

1. The States Parties to the present Covenant recognize the right of everyone:

(a) To take part in cultural life;

(b) To enjoy the benefits of scientific progress and its applications;

(c) To benefit from the protection of the moral and material interests resulting from any scientific, literary or artistic production of which he is the author.

2. The steps to be taken by the States Parties to the present Covenant to achieve the full realization of this right shall include those necessary for the conservation, the development and the diffusion of science and culture.

3. The States Parties to the present Covenant undertake to respect the freedom indispensable for scientific research and creative activity.

4. The States Parties to the present Covenant recognize the benefits to be derived from the encouragement and development of international contacts and co-operation in the scientific and cultural fields.

. . .

13. INTERNATIONAL COVENANT ON CIVIL AND POLITICAL RIGHTS[1]

Preamble

The States Parties to the present Covenant,

Considering that, in accordance with the principles proclaimed in the Charter of the United Nations, recognition of the inherent dignity and of the equal and inalienable rights of all members of the human family is the foundation of freedom, justice and peace in the world,

Recognizing that these rights derive from the inherent dignity of the human person,

Recognizing that, in accordance with the Universal Declaration of Human Rights, the ideal of free human beings enjoying civil and political freedom and freedom from fear and want can only be achieved if conditions are created whereby everyone may enjoy his civil and political rights, as well as his economic, social and cultural rights,

Considering the obligation of States under the Charter of the United Nations to promote universal respect for, and observance of, human rights and freedoms,

Realizing that the individual, having duties to other indiviudals and to the community to which he belongs, is under a responsibility to strive for the promotion and observance of the rights recognized in the present Covenant,

Agree upon the following articles:

. . .

[1]Adopted by 106 votes to none, with no abstentions, and opened for signature, ratification and accession by General Assembly reolution 2200 A (XXI) of 16 December 1966. Had not come into force on 1 July 1973.

Article 2

1. Each State Party to the present Covenant undertakes to respect and to ensure to all individuals within its territory and subject to its jurisdiction the rights recognized in the present Covenant, without distinction of any kind, such as race, colour, sex, language, religion, political or other opinion, national or social origin, property, birth or other status.

2. Where not already provided for by existing legislative or other measures, each State Party to the present Covenant undertakes to take the necessary steps, in accordance with its constitutional processes and with the provisions of the present Covenant, to adopt such legislative or other measures as may be necessary to give effect to the rights recognized in the present Covenant.

3. Each State Party to the present Covenant undertakes:

(a) To ensure that any person whose rights or freedoms as herein recognized are violated shall have an effective remedy, notwithstanding that the violation has been committed by persons acting in an official capacity;

(b) To ensure that any person claiming such a remedy shall have his right thereto determined by competent judicial, administrative or legislative authorities, or by any other competent authority provided for by the legal system of the State, and to develop the possibilities of judicial remedy;

(c) To ensure that the competent authorities shall enforce such remedies when granted.

Article 3

The States Parties to the present Covenant undertake to ensure the equal right of men and women to the enjoyment of all civil and political rights set forth in the present Covenant.

. . .

Article 5

. . .

2. There shall be no restriction upon or derogation from any of the fundamental human rights recognized or existing in any State Party to the present Covenant pursuant to law, conventions, regulations or custom on the pretext that the present Covenant does not recognize such rights or that it recognizes them to a lesser extent.

Article 6

1. Every human being has the inherent right to life. This right shall be protected by law. No one shall be arbitrarily deprived of his life.

. . .

Article 17

1. No one shall be subjected to arbitrary or unlawful interference with his privacy, family, home or correspondence, nor to unlawful attacks on his honour and reputation.

2. Everyone has the right to the protection of the law against such interference or attacks.

Article 18

1. Everyone shall have the right to freedom of thought, conscience and religion. This right shall include freedom to have or to adopt a religion or belief of his choice, and freedom, either individually or in community with others and in public or private, to manifest his religion or belief in worship, observance, practice and teaching.

2. No one shall be subject to coercion which would impair his freedom to have or to adopt a religion or belief of his choice.

3. Freedom to manifest one's religion or beliefs may be subject only to such limitations as are prescribed by law and are necessary to protect public safety, order, health, or morals or the fundamental rights and freedoms of others.

4. The States Parties to the present Covenant undertake to have respect for the liberty of parents and, when applicable, legal guardians to ensure the religious and moral education of their children in conformity with their own convictions.

Article 19

1. Everyone shall have the right to hold opinions without interference.

2. Everyone shall have the right to freedom of expression; this right shall include freedom to seek, receive and impart information and ideas of all kinds, regardless of frontiers, either orally, in writing or in print, in the form of art, or through any other media of his choice.

3. The exercise of the rights provided for in paragraph 2 of this article carries with it special duties and responsibilities. It may therefore be subject to certain restrictions, but these shall only be such as are provided by law and are necessary:

(a) For respect of the rights or reputations of others;

(b) For the protection of national security or of public order (*ordre public*), or of public health or morals.

. . .

Article 23

1. The family is the natural and fundamental group unit of society and is entitled to protection by society and the State.

2. The right of men and women of marriageable age to marry and to found a family shall be recognized.

3. No marriage shall be entered into without the free and full consent of the intending spouses.

4. States Parties to the present Covenant shall take appropriate steps to ensure equality of rights and responsibilities of spouses as to marriage, during marriage and at its dissolution. In the case of dissolution, provision shall be made for the necessary protection of any children.

Article 24

1. Every child shall have, without any discrimination as to race, colour, sex, language, religion, national or social origin, property or birth, the right to such measures of protection as are required by his status as a minor, on the part of his family, society and the State.

2. Every child shall be registered immediately after birth and shall have a name.

3. Every child has the right to acquire a nationality.

. . .

Article 26

All persons are equal before the law and are entitled without any discrimination to the equal protection of the law. In this respect, the law shall prohibit any discrimination and guarantee to all persons equal and effective protection against discrimination on any ground such as race, colour, sex, language, religion, political or other opinion, national or social origin, property, birth or other status.

Article 27

In those States in which ethnic, religious or linguistic minorities exist, persons belonging to such minorities shall not be denied the right, in community with the other members of their group, to enjoy their own culture, to profess and practice their own religion, or to use their own language.

. . .

14. DECLARATION ON THE ELIMINATION OF
DISCRIMINATION AGAINST WOMEN[1]

The General Assembly,

Considering that the peoples of the United Nations have, in the Charter, reaffirmed their faith in fundamental human rights, in the dignity

---

[1]Adopted unanimously and proclaimed under General Assembly reolution 2263 (XXII) of 7 November 1967.

and worth of the human person and in the equal rights of men and women,

Considering that the Universal Declaration of Human Rights asserts the principle of non-discrimination and proclaims that all human beings are born free and equal in dignity and rights and that everyone is entitled to all the rights and freedoms set forth therein, without distinction of any kind, including any distinction as to sex,

Taking into account the resolutions, declarations, conventions and recommendations of the United Nations and the specialized agencies designed to eliminate all forms of discrimination and to promote rights for men and women,

Concerned that, despite the Charter of the United Nations, the Universal Declaration of Human Rights, the International Covenants on Human Rights and other instruments of the United Nations and the specialized agencies and despite the progress made in the matter of equality of rights, there continues to exist considerable discrimination against women,

Considering that discrimination against women is incompatible with human dignity and with the welfare of the family and of society, prevents their participation, on equal terms with men, in the political, social, economic and cultural life of their countries and is an obstacle to the full development of the potentialities of women in the service of their countries and of humanity,

Bearing in mind the great contribution made by women to social, political, economic and cultural life and the part they play in the family and particularly in the rearing of children,

Convinced that the full and complete development of a country, the welfare of the world and the cause of peace require the maximum participation of women as well as men in all fields,

Considering that it is necessary to ensure the universal recognition in law and in fact of the principle of equality of men and women,

Solemnly proclaims this Declaration:

Article 1

Discrimination against women, denying or limiting as it does their equality of rights with men, is fundamentally unjust and constitutes an offence against human dignity.

Article 2

All appropriate measures shall be taken to abolish existing laws, customs, regulations and practices which are discriminatory against women, and to establish adequate legal protection for equal rights of men and women; in particular:

(a) The principle of equality of rights shall be embodied in the constitution or otherwise guaranteed by law;

(b) The international instruments of the United Nations and the specialized agencies relating to the elimination of discrimination against women shall be ratified or acceded to and fully implemented as soon as practicable.

. . .

Article 6

1. Without prejudice to the safeguarding of the unity and the harmony of the family, which remains the basic unit of any society, all appropriate measures, particularly legislative measures, shall be taken to ensure to women, married or unmarried, equal rights with men in the field of civil law, and in particular:

(a) The right to acquire, administer, enjoy, dispose of and inherit property, including property acquired during marriage;

(b) The right to equality in legal capacity and the exercise thereof;

(c) The same rights as men with regard to the law on the movement of persons.

2. All appropriate measures shall be taken to ensure the principle of equality of status of the husband and wife, and in particular:

(a) Women shall have the same right as men to free choice of a spouse and to enter into marriage only with their free and full consent;

(b) Women shall have equal rights with men during marriage and at its dissolution. In all cases the interest of the children shall be paramount;

(c) Parents shall have equal rights and duties in matters relating to their children. In all cases the interest of the children shall be paramount.

3. Child marriage and the betrothal of young girls before puberty shall be prohibited, and effective action, including legislation, shall be taken to specify a minimum age for marriage and to make the registration of marriages in an official registry compulsory.

. . .

Article 9

All appropriate measures shall be taken to ensure to girls and women, married or unmarried, equal rights with men in education at all levels, and in particular:

(a) Equal conditions of access to, and study in, educational institutions of all types, including universities and vocational, technical and professional schools;

(b) The same choice of curricula, the same examinations, teaching staff with qualifications of the same standard, and school premises and equipment of the same quality, whether the institutions are co-educational or not;

(c) Equal opportunities to benefit from scholarships and other study grants;

(d) Equal opportunities for access to programmes of continuing education, including adult literacy programmes;

(e) Access to educational information to help in ensuring the health and well-being of families.

Article 10

1. All appropriate measures shall be taken to ensure to women, married or unmarried, equal rights with men in the field of economic and social life, and in particular:

(a) The right, without discrimination on grounds of marital status or any other grounds, to receive vocational training, to work, to free choice of profession and employment, and to professional and vocational advancement;

(b) The right to equal remuneration with men and to equality of treatment in respect of work of equal value;

(c) The right to leave with pay, retirement privileges and provision for security in respect of unemployment, sickness, old age or other incapacity to work;

(d) The right to receive family allowances on equal terms with men.

2. In order to prevent discimination against women on account of marriage or maternity and to ensure their effective right to work, measures shall be taken to prevent their dismissal in the event of marriage or maternity and to provide paid maternity leave, with the guarantee of returning to former employment, and to provide the necessary social services, including child-care facilities.

. . .

15. FINAL ACT OF THE INTERNATIONAL CONFERENCE
ON HUMAN RIGHTS, TEHERAN, 1968

A. PROCLAMATION OF TEHERAN[1]

The International Conference on Human Rights,

Having met at Teheran from April 22 to May 13, 1968 to review the progress made in the twenty years since the adoption of the Universal Declaration of Human Rights and to formulate a programme for the future,

---

[1]Adopted without objection, 13 May 1968, at the International Conference on Human Rights, held at Teheran, 22 April to 13 May 1968.

Having considered the problems relating to the activities of the United Nations for the promotion and encouragement of respect for human rights and fundamental freedoms,

Bearing in mind the resolutions adopted by the Conference,

Noting that the observance of the International Year for Human Rights takes place at a time when the world is undergoing a process of unprecedented change,

Having regard to the new opportunities made available by the rapid progress of science and technology,

Believing that, in an age when conflict and violence prevail in many parts of the world, the fact of human interdependence and the need for human solidarity are more evident than ever before,

Recognizing that peace is the universal aspiration of mankind and that peace and justice are indispensable to the full realization of human rights and fundamental freedoms,

Solemnly proclaims that:

. . .

13. Since human rights and fundamental freedoms are indivisible, the full realization of civil and political rights without the enjoyment of economic, social and cultural rights is impossible. The achievement of lasting progress in the implementation of human rights is dependent upon sound and effective national and international policies of economic and social development;

14. The existence of over seven hundred million illiterates throughout the world is an enormous obstacle to all efforts at realizing the aims and purposes of the Charter of the United Nations and the provisions of the Universal Declaration of Human Rights. International action aimed at eradicating illiteracy from the face of the earth and promoting education at all levels requires urgent attention;

15. The discrimination of which women are still victims in various regions of the world must be eliminated. An inferior status for women is contrary to the Charter of the United Nations as well as the provisions of the Universal Declaration of Human Rights. The full implementation of the Declaration on the Elimination of All Forms of Discrimination Against Women is a necessity for the progress of mankind;

16. The protection of the family and of the child remains the concern of the international community. Parents have a basic human right to determine freely and responsibly the number and the spacing of their children;

. . .

B. HUMAN RIGHTS ASPECTS OF FAMILY PLANNING[1]

The International Conference on Human Rights

Recalling the determination of the peoples of the United Nations, as expressed in the Charter, to reaffirm faith in fundamental human rights, in the dignity and worth of the human person, in the equal rights of men and women and of nations large and small, and to promote social progress and better standards of life in larger freedom,

Considering that article 16 of the Universal Declaration of Human Rights states *inter alia* that men and women of full age have the right to marry and found a family and that the family is the natural and fundamental group of society,

Recalling General Assembly resolution 2211 (XXI) of 17 December 1966, which recognized *inter alia* the sovereignty of nations in formulating and promoting their own population policies, with due regard to the principle that the size of the family should be the free choice of each individual family,

Recalling also UNESCO resolution 3.252 of 14 December 1966, the World Health Assembly's resolution WHA 20.41 of 25 May 1967 and the conclusions of the World Population Conference held at Belgrade in September 1965 on the subject of family planning,

Noting with interest that the Commission on the Status of Women has begun to study the relationship between family planning and the status of women,

Noting also the Declaration on Population of 10 December 1966, now signed by 30 Heads of State or Government,

Believing that it is timely to draw attention to the connexion between population growth and human rights,

1. *Observes* that the present rapid rate of population growth in some areas of the world hampers the struggle against hunger and poverty, and in particular reduces the possibilities of rapidly achieving adequate standards of living, including food, clothing, housing, medical care, social security, education and social services, thereby impairing the full realization of human rights;

2. *Recognizes* that moderation of the present rate of population growth in such areas would enhance the conditions for offering greater opportunities for the enjoyment of human rights and the improvement of living conditions for each person;

3. *Considers* that couples have a basic human right to decide freely and responsibly on the number and spacing of their children and a right

---

[1]Resolution XVIII of the International Conference on Human Rights held at Teheran, 22 April to 13 May 1968, adopted by 56 votes to none, with 7 abstentions.

to adequate education and information in this respect;

4. *Urges* Member States and United Nations bodies and specialized agencies concerned to give close attention to the implications for the exercise of human rights of the present rapid rate of increase in world population.

16. DECLARATION ON SOCIAL PROGRESS AND DEVELOPMENT[1]

The General Assembly,

Mindful of the pledge of Members of the United Nations under the Charter to take joint and separate action in cooperation with the Organization to promote higher standards of living, full employment and conditions of economic and social progress and development,

Reaffirming faith in human rights and fundamental freedoms and in the principles of peace, of the dignity and worth of the human person, and of social justice proclaimed in the Charter,

Recalling the principles of the Universal Declaration of Human Rights, the International Covenants on Human Rights, the Declaration of the Rights of the Child, the Declaration on the Granting of Independence to Colonial Countries and Peoples, the International Convention on the Elimination of All Forms of Racial Discrimination, the United Nations Declaration on the Elimination of All Forms of Racial Discrimination, the Declaration on the Promotion among Youth of the Ideals of Peace, Mutual Respect and Understanding between Peoples, the Declaration on the Elimination of Discrimination against Women and of resolutions of the United Nations,

Bearing in mind the standards already set for social progress in the constitutions, conventions, recommendations and resolutions of the International Labour Organisation, the Food and Agriculture Organization of the United Nations, the United Nations Educational, Scientific and Cultural Organization, the World Health Organization, the United Nations Children's Fund and of other organizations concerned,

Convinced that man can achieve complete fulfilment of his aspirations only within a just social order and that it is consequently of cardinal importance to accelerate social and economic progress everywhere, thus contributing to international peace and solidarity,

Convinced that international peace and security on the one hand, and social progress and economic development on the other, are closely interdependent and influence each other,

---

[1] Adopted by 119 votes to none, with 2 abstentions, and proclaimed under General Assembly resolution 2542 (XXIV) of 11 December 1969.

Persuaded that social development can be promoted by peaceful co-existence, friendly relations and cooperation among States with different social, economic or political systems,

Emphasizing the interdependence of economic and social development in the wider process of growth and change, as well as the importance of a strategy of integrated development which takes full account at all stages of its social aspects,

Regretting the inadequate progress achieved in the world social situation despite the efforts of States and the international community,

Recognizing that the primary responsibility for the development of the developing countries rests on those countries themselves and acknowledging the pressing need to narrow and eventually close the gap in the standards of living between economically more advanced and developing countries and, to that end, that Member States shall have the responsibility to pursue internal and external policies designed to promote social development throughout the world, and in particular to assist developing countries to accelerate their economic growth,

Recognizing the urgency of devoting to works of peace and social progress resources being expended on armaments and wasted on conflict and destruction,

Conscious of the contribution that science and technology can render towards meeting the needs common to all humanity,

Believing that the primary task of all States and international organizations is to eliminate from the life of society all evils and obstacles to social progress, particularly such evils as inequality, exploitation, war, colonialism and racism,

Desirous of promoting the progress of all mankind towards these goals and of overcoming all obstacles to their realization,

Solemnly proclaims this Declaration on Social Progress and Development and calls for national and international action for its use as a common basis for social development policies:

Part I

Principles

Article 1

All peoples and all human beings, without distinction as to race, colour, sex, language, religion, nationality, ethnic origin, family or social status, or political or other conviction, shall have the right to live in dignity and freedom and to enjoy the fruits of social progress and should, on their part, contribute to it.

. . .

Article 4

The family as a basic unit of society and the natural environment for the growth and well-being of all its members, particularly children and youth, should be assisted and protected so that it may fully assume its responsibilities within the community. Parents have the exclusive right to determine freely and responsibly the number and spacing of their children.

Article 5

Social progress and development require the full utilization of human resources, including, in particular:

(a) The encouragement of creative initiative under conditions of enlightened public opinion;

(b) The dissemination of national and international information for the purpose of making individuals aware of changes occurring in society as a whole;

(c) The active participation of all elements of society, individually or through associations, in defining and in achieving the common goals of development with full respect for the fundamental freedoms embodied in the Universal Declaration of Human Rights;

(d) The assurance to disadvantaged or marginal sectors of the population of equal opportunities for social and economic advancement in order to achieve an effectively integrated society.

. . .

PART II

Objectives

Social progress and development shall aim at the continuous raising of the material and spiritual standards of living of all members of society, with respect for and in compliance with human rights and fundamental freedoms, through the attainment of the following main goals:

Article 10

(a) The assurance at all levels of the right to work and the right of everyone to form trade unions and workers' associations and to bargain collectively; promotion of full productive employment and elimination of unemployment and under-employment; establishment of equitable and favourable conditions of work for all, including the improvement of health and safety conditions; assurance of just remuneration for labour without any discrimination as well as a sufficiently high minimum wage to ensure a decent standard of living; the protection of the consumer;

(b) The elimination of hunger and malnutrition and the guarantee of the right to proper nutrition;

(c) The elimination of poverty; the assurance of a steady improvement in levels of living and of a just and equitable distribution of income;

(d) The achievement of the highest standards of health and the provision of health protection for the entire population, if possible free of charge;

(e) The eradication of illiteracy and the assurance of the right to universal access to culture, to free compulsory education at the elementary level and to free education at all levels; the raising of the general level of life-long education;

(f) The provision for all, particularly persons in low-income groups and large families, of adequate housing and community services. Social progress and development shall aim equally at the progressive attainment of the following main goals:

Article 11

(a) The provision of comprehensive social security schemes and social welfare services; the establishment and improvement of social security and insurance schemes for all persons who, because of illness, disability or old age, are temporarily or permanently unable to earn a living, with a view to ensuring a proper standard of living for such persons and for their families and dependants;

(b) The protection of the rights of the mother and child; concern for the upbringing and health of children; the provision of measures to safeguard the health and welfare of women and particularly of working mothers during pregnancy and the infancy of their children, as well as of mothers whose earnings are the sole source of livelihood for the family; the granting to women of pregnancy and maternity leave and allowances without loss of employment or wages;

(c) The protection of the rights and the assuring of the welfare of children, the aged and the disabled; the provision of protection for the physically or mentally disadvanteaged;

(d) The education of youth in, and promotion among them of, the ideals of justice and peace, mutual respect and understanding among peoples; the promotion of full participation of youth in the process of national development;

. . .

Part III

Means and Methods

On the basis of the principles set forth in this Declaration, the achievement of the objectives of social progress and development requires the

mobilization of the necessary resources by national and international action, with particular attention to such means and methods as:
. . .

Article 17

(a) The adoption of measures to accelerate the process of industrialization, especially in developing countries, with due regard for its social aspects, in the interests of the entire population; development of an adequate organizational and legal framework conducive to an uninterrupted and diversified growth of the industrial sector; measures to overcome the adverse social effects which may result from urban development and industrialization, including automation; maintenance of a proper balance between rural and urban development, and in particular, measures designed to ensure healthier living conditions, especially in large industrial centres;

(b) Integrated planning to meet the problems of urbanization and urban development;

(c) Comprehensive rural development schemes to raise the levels of living of the rural populations and to facilitate such urban-rural relationships and population distribtuion as will promote balanced national development and social progress;

(d) Measures for appropriate supervision of the utilization of land in the interests of society.
. . .

Article 19

(a) The provision of free health services to the whole population and of adequate preventive and curative facilities and welfare medical services accessible to all;

(b) The enactment and establishment of legislative measures and administrative regulations with a view to the implementation of comprehensive programmes of social security schemes and social welfare services and to the improvement and coordination of existing services;

(c) The adoption of measures and the provision of social welfare services to migrant workers and their families, in conformity with the provisions of Convention No. 97 of the International Labour Organisation and other international instruments relating to migrant workers;

(d) The institution of appropriate measures for the rehabilitation of mentally or physically disabled persons, especially children and youth, so as to enable them to the fullest possible extent to be useful members of society — these measures shall include the provision of treatment and technical appliances, education, vocational and social guidance, training and selective placement, and other assistance required — and the creation of social conditions in which the handicapped are not discriminated against because of their disabilities.

. . .

Article 22

(a) The development and coordination of policies and measures designed to strengthen the essential functions of the family as a basic unit of society;

(b) The formulation and establishment, as needed, of programmes in the field of population, within the framework of national demographic policies and as part of the welfare medical services, including education, training of personnel and the provision to families of the knowledge and means necessary to enable them to exercise their right to determine freely and responsibly the number and spacing of their children;

(c) The establishment of appropriate child-care facilities in the interest of children and working parents.

. . .

17. INTERNATIONAL DEVELOPMENT STRATEGY FOR THE SECOND UNITED NATIONS DEVELOPMENT DECADE: 2626 (XXV)[1]

The General Assembly

1. *Proclaims* the Second United Nations Development Decade starting from 1 January 1971;

2. *Adopts* the following International Development Strategy for the Decade:

. . .

B. GOALS AND OBJECTIVES

(13) The average annual rate of growth in the gross product of the developing countries as a whole during the Second United Nations Development Decade should be at least 6 per cent, with the possibility of attaining a higher rate in the second half of the Decade to be specified on the basis of a comprehensive mid-term review. This target and those derived from it are a broad indication of the scope of convergent efforts to be made during the Decade at the national and international levels; it should be the responsibility of each developing country to set its own target for growth in the light of its own circumstances.

---

[1]Adopted without a vote and proclaimed under General Assembly resolution 2626 (XXV) of 24 October 1970.

(14) The average annual rate of growth of gross product per head in developing countries as a whole during the Decade should be about 3.5 per cent with the possibility of accelerating it during the second half of the Decade in order at least to make a modest beginning towards narrowing the gap in living standards between developed and developing countries. An average annual growth rate of 3.5 per cent per head will represent a doubling of average income per head in the course of two decades. In countries with very low incomes per head, efforts should be made to double such incomes within a shorter period.

(15) The target for growth in average income per head is calculated on the basis of an average annual increase of 2.5 per cent in the population of developing countries, which is less than the average rate at present forecast for the 1970s. In this context, each developing country should formulate its own demographic objectives within the framwork of its national development plan.

(16) An average annual rate of growth of at least 6 per cent in the gross product of developing countries during the Decade will imply an average annual expanision of:

(a) 4 per cent in agricultural output;

(b) 8 per cent in manufacturing output.

(17) For attaining the over-all growth target of at least 6 per cent *per annum*, there should be an average annual expansion of:

(a) 0.5 per cent in the ratio of gross domestic saving to the gross product so that this ratio rises to around 20 per cent by 1980;

(b) Somewhat less than 7 per cent in imports and somewhat higher than 7 per cent in exports.

(18) As the ultimate purpose of development is to provide increasing opportunities to all people for a better life, it is essential to bring about a more equitable distribution of income and wealth for promoting both social justice and efficiency of production, to raise substantially the level of employment, to achieve a greater degree of income security, to expand and improve facilities for education, health, nutrition, housing and social welfare, and to safeguard the environment. Thus, qualitative and structural changes in the society must go hand in hand with rapid economic growth, and existing disparities — regional, sectoral and social — should be substantially reduced. These objectives are both determining factors and end-results of development; they should therefore be viewed as integrated parts of the same dynamic process and would require a unified approach:

(a) Each developing country should formulate its national employment objectives so as to absorb an increasing proportion of its working population in modern-type activities and to reduce significantly unemployment and underemployment;

(b) Particular attention should be paid to achieving enrollment of all children of primary school age, improvement in the quality of education at all levels, a substantial reduction in illiteracy, the reorientation of educational programmes to serve development needs and, as appropriate, the establishment and expansion of scientific and technological institutions;

(c) Each developing country should formulate a coherent health programme for the prevention and treatment of diseases and for raising general levels of health and sanitation;

(d) Levels of nutrition should be improved in terms of the average caloric intake and the protein content, with special emphasis being placed on the needs of vulnerable groups of population;

(e) Housing facilities should be expanded and improved, especially for the low-income groups and with a view to remedying the ills of unplanned urban growth and lagging rural areas.

(f) The well-being of children should be fostered;

(g) The full participation of youth in the development process should be ensured;

(h) The full integration of women in the total development effort should be encouraged.

C. Policy Measures

(19) The above goals and objectives call for a continuing effort by all peoples and Governments to promote economic and social progress in developing countries by the formulation and implementation of a coherent set of policy measures. Animated by a spirit of constructive partnership and cooperation, based on the interdependence of their interests and designed to promote a rational system of international division of labour, and reflecting their political will and collective determination to achieve these goals and objectives, Governments, individually and jointly, solemnly resolve to adopt and implement the policy measures set out below.

(20) The policy measures should be viewed in a dynamic context, involving continuing review to ensure their effective implementation and adaptation in the light of new developments, including the far-reaching impact of rapid advance in technology, and to seek new areas of agreement and the widening of the existing ones. Organizations of the United Nations system will appropriately assist in the implementation of these measures and in the search for new avenues of international cooperation for development.

. . .

7. Science and technology

(60) Concerted efforts will be made by the developing countries, with appropriate assistance from the rest of the world community, to expand their capability to apply science and technology for development so as to enable the technological gap to be significantly reduced.

(61) Developing countries will continue to increase their expenditure on research and development and will endeavour to attain, by the end of the Decade, a minimum average level equivalent to 0.5 per cent of their gross product. They will endeavour to inculcate, among their people, an appreciation of the scientific approach which will influence all their development policies. The research programme will be oriented to the development of technologies that are in line with the circumstances and requirements of individual countries and regions. They will put particular stress on applied research and seek to develop the basic infrastructure of science and technology.

(62) Full international cooperation will be extended for the establishment, strengthening and promotion of scientific research and technological activities which have a bearing on the expansion and modernization of the economies of developing countries. Particular attention will be devoted to fostering technologies suitable for these countries. Concentrated research efforts will be made in relation to selected problems the solutions to which can have a catalytic effect in accelerating development. Assistance will also be provided for building up and, as appropriate, for expanding and improving research institutions in developing countries, expecially on a regional or subregional basis. Efforts will be made to promote close cooperation between the scientific work and staff of the research centres in developing countries and between those in developed and developing countries.

(63) Within the framework of their individual aid and technical assistance programmes, developed countries will substantially increase their aid for the direct support of science and technology in developing countries during the Decade. Consideration will be given to the question of setting a target equivalent to a specified percentage of the gross national product of developed countries at the time of the first biennial review, taking fully into account the relevant factors. Moreover the developed countries will, in their research and development programmes, assist in seeking solutions to the specific problems of developing countries and for this purpose will endeavour to provide adequate resources. Serious consideration will be given during the first biennial review to the question of setting a specified target in this field. Developed countries will make all efforts to incur in developing countries a significant proportion of their research and development expenditure on specific problems of developing countries. In cooperation with the developing countries, devel-

oped countries will continue to explore the possibility of locating some of their research and development projects in developing countries. Private foundations, institutions and organizations will be encouraged to provide further assistance for expanding and diversifying research activities of benefit to developing countries. In relation to their aid and investment policies, developed countries will assist developing countries in identifying technologies which are appropriate for their circumstances and in avoiding the utilization of scarce resources for inappropriate technologies.

(64) Developed and developing countries and competent international organizations will draw up and implement a programme for promoting the transfer of technology to developing countries, which will include, *inter alia,* the review of international conventions on patents, the identification and reduction of obstacles to the transfer of technology to developing countries, facilitating access to patented and non-patented technology for developing countries under fair and reasonable terms and conditions, facilitating the utilization of technology transferred to developing countries in such a manner as to assist these countries in attaining their trade and development objectives, the development of technology suited to the productive structure of developing countries and measures to accelerate the development of indigenous technology.

8. Human development

(65) Those developing countires which consider that their rate of population growth hampers their development will adopt measures which they deem necessary in accordance with their concept of development. Developed countries, consistent with their national policies, will upon request provide support through the supply of means for family planning and further research. International organizations concerned will continue to provide, when appropriate, the assistance that may be requested by interested Governments. Such support or assistance will not be a substitute for other forms of development assistance.

(66) Developing countries will make vigorous efforts to improve labour force statistics in order to be able to formulate realistic quantitative targets for employment. They will scrutinize their fiscal, monetary, trade and other policies with a view to promoting both employment and growth. Moreover, for achieving these objectives they will expand their investment through a fuller mobilization of domestic resources and an increased flow of assistance from abroad. Wherever a choice of technology is available, developing countries will seek to raise the level of employment by ensuring that capital-intensive technology is confined to uses in which it is clearly cheaper in real terms and more efficient. Developed countries will assist in this process by adopting measures to bring about

appropriate changes in the structures of international trade. As part of their employment strategy, developing countries will put as much emphasis as possible on rural employment and will also consider undertaking public works that harness manpower which would otherwise remain unutilized. These countries will also strengthen institutions able to contribute to constructive industrial relations policies and appropriate labour standards. Developed countries and international organizations will assist developing countries in attaining their employment objectives.

(67) Developing countries will formulate and implement educational programmes taking into account their development needs. Educational and training programmes will be so designed as to increase productivity substantially in the short run and to reduce waste. Particular emphasis will be placed on teacher-training programmes and on the development of curriculum materials to be used by teachers. As appropriate, curricula will be revised and new approaches initiated in order to ensure at all levels expansion of skills in line with the rising tempo of activities and the accelerating transformations brought about by technological progress. Increasing use will be made of modern equipment, mass media and new teaching methods to improve the efficiency of education. Particular attention will be devoted to technical training, vocational training and retraining. Necessary facilities will be provided for improving the literacy and technical competence of groups that are already productively engaged as well as for adult education. Developed countries and international institutions will assist in the task of extending and improving the systems of education of developing countries, especially by making available some of the educational inputs in short supply in many developing countries and by providing assistance to facilitate the flow of pedagogic resources among them.

(68) Developing countries will establish at least a minimum programme of health facilities comprising an infrastructure of institutions, including those for medical training and research to bring basic medical services within the reach of a specified proportion of their population by the end of the Decade. These will include basic health services for the prevention and treatment of diseases and for the promotion of health. Each developing country will endeavour to provide an adequate supply of potable water to a specified proportion of its population, both urban and rural, with a view to reaching a minimum target by the end of the Decade. Efforts of the developing countries to raise their levels of health will be supported to the maximum feasible extent by developed countries, particularly through assistance in the planning of health promotion strategy and the implementation of some of its segments, including research, training of personnel at all levels and supply of equipment and medicines. A concerted international effort will be made to mount a

world-wide campaign to eradicate by the end of the Decade, from as many countries as possible, one or more diseases that still seriously afflict people in many lands. Developed countries and international organizations will assist the developing countries in their health planning and in the establishment of health institutions.

(69) Developing countries will adopt policies consistent with their agricultural and health programmes in an effort towards meeting their nutritional requirements. These will include development and production of high-protein foods and development and wider use of new forms of edible protein. Financial and technical assistance, including assistance for genetic research, will be extended to them by developed countries and international institutions.

(70) Developing countries will adopt suitable national policies for involving children and youth in the development process and for ensuring that their needs are met in an integrated manner.

(71) Developing countries will take steps to provide improved housing and related community facilities in both urban and rural areas, especially for low-income groups. They will also seek to remedy the ills of unplanned urbanization and to undertake necessary town planning. Particular effort will be made to expand low-cost housing through both public and private programmes and on a self-help basis, and also through cooperatives, utilizing as much as possible local raw materials and labour-intensive techniques. Appropriate international assistance will be provided for this purpose.

(72) Governments will intensify national and international efforts to arrest the deterioration of the human environment and to take measures towards its improvement, and to promote activities that will help to maintain the ecological balance on which human survival depends.

. . .

18. DECLARATION OF THE UNITED NATIONS CONFERENCE
     ON THE HUMAN ENVIRONMENT[1]

The United Nations Conference on the Human Environment

Having met at Stockholm from 5 to 16 June 1972.

Having considered the need for a common outlook and for common principles to inspire and guide the peoples of the world in the preservation and enhancement of the human environment.

---

[1]Adopted by the Conference as a whole subject to the observations and reservations made by members of the Conference.

I

Proclaims that

1. Man is both creature and moulder of his environment, which gives him physical sustenance and affords him the opportunity for intellectual, moral, social and spiritual growth. In the long and tortuous evolution of the human race on this planet a stage has been reached when, through the rapid acceleration of science and technology, man has acquired the power to transform his environment in countless ways and on an unprecedented scale. Both aspects of man's environment, the natural and the man-made, are essential to his well-being and to the enjoyment of basic human rights — even the right to life itself.

2. The protection and improvement of the human environment is a major issue which affects the well-being of peoples and economic development throughout the world; it is the urgent desire of the peoples of the whole world and the duty of all Governments.

3. Man has constantly to sum up experience and go on discovering, inventing, creating and advancing. In our time, man's capability to transform his surroundings, if used wisely, can bring to all peoples the benefits of development and the opportunity to enhance the quality of life. Wrongly or heedlessly applied, the same power can do incalculable harm to human beings and the human environment. We see around us growing evidence of man-made harm in many regions of the earth: dangerous levels of pollution in water, air, earth and living beings; major and undesirable disturbances to the ecological balance of the biosphere; destruction and depletion of irreplaceable resources; and gross deficiencies harmful to the physical, mental and social health of man, in the man-made environment, particularly in the living and working environment.

4. In the developing countries most of the environmental problems are caused by underdevelopment. Millions continue to live far below the minimum levels required for a decent human existence, deprived of adequate food and clothing, shelter and education, health and sanitation. Therefore, the developing countries must direct their efforts to development, bearing in mind their priorities and the need to safeguard and improve the environment. For the same purpose, the industrialized countries should make efforts to reduce the gap between themselves and the developing countries. In the industrialized countries, environmental problems are generally related to industrialization and technological development.

5. The natural growth of population continuously presents problems for the preservation of the environment, and adequate policies and measures should be adopted, as appropriate, to face these problems. Of all things in the world, people are the most precious. It is the people that propel social progress, create social wealth, develop science and technol-

ogy and, through their hard work, continuously transform the human environment. Along with social progress and the advance of production, science and technology, the capability of man to improve the environment increases with each passing day.

6. A point has been reached in history when we must shape our actions throughout the world with a more prudent care for their environmental consequences. Through ignorance or indifference we can do massive and irreversible harm to the earthly environment on which our life and well-being depend. Conversely, through fuller knowledge and wiser action, we can achieve for ourselves and our posterity a better life in an environment more in keeping with human needs and hopes. There are broad vistas for the enhancement of environmental quality and the creation of a good life. What is needed is an enthusiastic but calm state of mind and intense but orderly work. For the purpose of attaining freedom in the world of nature, man must use knowledge to build, in collaboration with nature, a better environment. To defend and improve the human environment for present and future generations has become an imperative goal for mankind — a goal to be pursued together with, and in harmony with, the established and fundamental goals of peace and of world-wide economic and social development.

7. To achieve this environmental goal will demand the acceptance of responsibility by citizens and communities, and by enterprises and institutions at every level, all sharing equitably in common efforts. Individuals in all walks of life as well as organizations in many fields, by their values and the sum of their actions, will shape the world environment of the future. Local and national governments will bear the greatest burden for large-scale environmental policy and action within their jurisdictions. International cooperation is also needed in order to raise resources to support the developing countries in carrying out their responsibilities in this field. A growing class of environmental problems, because they are regional or global in extent or because they affect the common international realm, will require extensive cooperation among nations and action by international organizations in the common interest. The Conference calls upon Governments and peoples to exert common efforts for the preservation and improvement of the human environment, for the benefit of all the people and for their posterity.

II

Principles

States the common conviction that

Principle 1.

Man has the fundamental right to freedom, equality and adequate conditions of life, in an environment of a quality that permits a life of dignity and well-being, and he bears a solemn responsibility to protect and improve the environment for present and future generations.

. . .

Principle 8.

Economic and social development is essential for ensuring a favourable living and working environment for man and for creating conditions on earth that are necessary for the improvement of the quality of life.

. . .

Principle 13.

In order to achieve a more rational management of resources and thus to improve the environment, States should adopt an integrated and co-ordinated approach to their development planning so as to ensure that development is compatible with the need to protect and improve the human environment for the benefit of their population.

Principle 14.

Rational planning constitutes an essential tool for reconciling any conflict between the needs of development and the need to protect and improve the environment.

Principle 15.

Planning must be applied to human settlements and urbanization with a view to avoiding adverse effects on the environment and obtaining maximum social, economic and environmental benefits for all. In this respect projects which are designed for colonialist and racist domination must be abandoned.

Principle 16

Demographic policies, which are without prejudice to basic human rights and which are deemed appropriate by Governments concerned, should be applied in those regions where the rate of population growth or excessive population concentrations are likely to have adverse effects on the environment or development, or where low population density may prevent improvement of the human environment and impede development.

. . .

Principle 19.

Education in environmental matters, for the younger generation as well as adults, giving due consideration to the underprivileged, is essential in order to broaden the basis for an enlightened opinion and responsible conduct by individuals, enterprises and communities in protecting and improving the environment in its full human dimension. It is also essential that mass media of communications avoid contributing to the deterioration of the environment, but, on the contrary, disseminate information of an educational nature, on the need to protect and improve the environment in order to enable man to develop in every respect.

. . .

19. DECLARATION OF POPULATION STRATEGY FOR DEVELOPMENT[1]

The Second Asian Population Conference,

Having considered the necessity of formulating population policies and programmes as integral parts of the social and economic development process,

Recognizing the urgent necessity of succeeding in efforts for economic and social development for the benefit of the countries and the greater welfare and happiness of all the peoples of the ECAFE region,

Recognizing the human right of every couple to determine freely and responsibly the number and spacing of their children and the need to ensure their access to information, education and the means so to do, no matter what their financial or social condition,

Recognizing further the social and economic impact of individual family size on societies, and considering it appropriate for Governments to take social and economic measures, in addition to family planning programmes, that will make a smaller family more acceptable and beneficial to the individual couple,

Giving full recognition to national sovereignties and to the need for each country to consider the establishment of goals and programmes for an effective control of the growth of population in the light of individual national conditions and policies,

Reaffirming the importance of integrating population into the development strategy of the Second United Nations Development Decade,

Taking note of the Stockholm Declaration and stressing the impact that rapid population growth has on the human environment,

Having considered the fields of concern identified in the report of the present Conference,

Desirous of ensuring that the World Population Conference and the World Population Year contribute their utmost towards the unviersal resolution of the problems of population and development, bearing in mind the inherent differences in such problems from country to country, and

---

[1]Adopted by the Second Asian Population Conference, at Tokyo, on 13 November 1972.

Emphasizing that the urgency of problems of population growth and distribution calls for intensive and dedicated work in various government sectors as well as innovative changes in many fields,

Declares that

1. While population has a direct effect on economic and social development and the human environment, conversely policies in the fields of education, health, housing, social security, employment and agriculture have an impact on population and, therefore, require integrated national planning and coordinating action at the highest government level.

2. It is important that the widespread benefits of economic growth should be ensured through policies and programmes to bring about a more equitable distribution of opportunity and income, with particular attention being paid to health and nutrition programmes to reduce infant and maternal mortality, programmes to achieve full and productive employment, action to reduce excessive rates of migration to the larger cities, measures to improve the status of women, and appropriate social security measures.

3. The priority of population and family planning fields should be recognized through the allocation of broad responsibilities in planning, evaluation and analysis of programmes in these fields to an appropriate organization within the governments.

4. Governments of the region which seek to fulfil the ideals of their people and their national goals through population policies and programmes should:

(a) recognize the essential role of population and family planning programmes as a means of effectively achieving the aspirations of families and their societies and should provide information, education and services for all citizens as early as possible.

(b) encourage small families in rural and urban areas through intensive efforts in information and education, with the help of all relevant institutions and resources and the enactment of appropriate social and economic measures;

(c) include in population policy and programmes provisions to ensure that all pertinent information reaches the policy-makers, opinion leaders, and socio-economic planners;

(d) encourage the development of new tools of communication and the utilization of existing ones so that knowledge may be shared at all levels of society;

(e) consider establishing population commissions or other bodies having multi-disciplinary and multi-departmental representation, to assess the current status and future needs in the fields of population and family planning;

(f) ensure coordination among various agencies at the national, regional and local levels in order to expedite action and plans formulated in the light of integrated development policies;

(g) provide essential training facilities with a view to improving planning skills, promoting comprehensive and innovative population policies and improving management skills in order to increase the administrative capabilities of population and family planning programmes.

5. The Economic Commission for Asia and the Far East (ECAFE) with the cooperation of the United Nations Fund for Population Activities (UNFPA) and other United Nations bodies, should ensure that there are, within the region, facilities for training and research in the fields of population and development, to meet the countries' needs for people skilled in the various areas of policy formulation, planning, implementation and evaluation, and to promote the advancement of knowledge in these fields.

6. The problems encountered in dealing with rapid population growth are of vital concern to the entire world community, and the Second Asian Population Conference requests that the report of its deliberations be taken into consideration in the drafting of the World Population Plan of Action; it likewise calls upon the World Population Conference, in 1974, to consider the means which might be applied on a global level for the solution of these problems.

7. Leadership and assistance on the part of the United Nations and its associated agencies are of crucial importance to all countries in achieving population goals consistent with and fundamental to the purposes set forth in this Declaration.

PART THREE

GENERAL ASSEMBLY RESOLUTIONS

PART III.
GENERAL ASSEMBLY RESOLUTIONS

1. CONVENTION ON THE PREVENTION AND PUNISHMENT OF THE CRIME OF GENOCIDE: 260 A (III). (SEE UNDER PART II ABOVE)

2. UNIVERSAL DECLARATION OF HUMAN RIGHTS: 217 (III) (SEE UNDER PART II ABOVE)

3. EXPANDED PROGRAMME OF TECHNICAL ASSISTANCE: 304 (IV)[1]

The General Assembly,

Having considered the Economic and Social Council's resolution 222(IX)A of 15 August 1949 on an expanded programme of technical assistance for economic development,

1. *Approves* the observations and guiding principles set out in annex I of that resolution and the arrangements made by the Council for the administration of the programme;

2. *Notes* the decision of the Council to call a Technical Assistance Conference to be convened by the Secretary-General in accordance with the terms of paragraphs 12 and 13 of the Council resolution;

3. *Authorizes* the Secretary-General to set up a special account for technical assistance for economic development, to be available to those organizations which participate in the expanded programme of technical assistance and which accept the observations and guiding principles set out in annex I of the Council resolution and the arrangements made by the Council for the administration of the programme;

4. *Approves* the recommendations of the Council to Governments participating in the Technical Assistance Conference regarding financial arrangements for administering contributions, and authorizes the Secretary-General to fulfill the responsibilities assigned to him in this connection;

5. *Invites* all Governments to make as large voluntary contributions as possible to the special account for technical assistance.

---

[1]Adopted unanimously, 16 November, 1949.

4. ADVISORY SOCIAL WELFARE SERVICES: 418 (V)[1]

The General Assembly,

Having considered the modifications made, in the light of General Assembly resolution 316 (IV), by the Economic and Social Council, in General Assembly resolution 58 (I) on advisory and social welfare services,

Approves the following text of resolution 58 (I) revised by the Economic and Social Council and amended by the Third Committee:

"*Whereas* by Articles 55 and 60 of the Charter of the United Nations, the Economic and Social Council, under the authority of the General Assembly, is charged with the responsibility for promoting higher standards of living and conditions of social progress and development,

"*Whereas* by Article 66 of the Charter, the Economic and Social Council may, with the approval of the General Assembly, perform services at the request of Members of the United Nations and at the request of specialized agencies,

"*Whereas* the General Assembly, after examining the recommendations of the Economic and Social Council and the accompanying report of services rendered for the first three years of operation, approved the recommendations and placed the advisory social welfare services originally authorized by resolution 58 (I) on a continuing basis, and requested that a review be made of the terms of that resolution and appropriate recommendations made with respect to desirable or necessary changes (resolution 316 (IV)),

"*Whereas* the General Assembly recognizes that the advisory social welfare services constitute a practical operational programme of direct assistance to Governments and that the other activities of the United Nations in the social field should be properly correlated with these services in order to achieve maximum effectiveness, to which end the Social Commission has adjusted its long-range work programme,

"*The General Assembly, therefore,*

"A. *Authorizes* the Secretary-General:

"1. Subject to the directions of the Economic and Social Council, to make provision for the undermentioned functions and services, such provision to be made, where appropriate, with the co-operation of the specialized agencies and in consultation with non-governmental organizations having consultative status:

"(a) For a requisite number of social welfare experts to provide advisory services at the request of Governments which show the need for them, and to put into practice, over an appropriate period, new methods in any branch of social welfare;

---

[1] Adopted unanimously, 1 December 1950.

"(b) For enabling suitably qualified social welfare officials to observe, and familiarize themselves with, the experience and practice of other countries in any branch of social welfare;

"(c) For enabling suitably qualified persons who cannot receive professional training in branches of social welfare in their own country to receive appropriate training in foreign countries having the necessary facilities;

"(d) For planning by appropriate methods projects for experimenting in or demonstrating various phases of social welfare, organizing and participating in these projects, providing the necessary tools and equipment in connexion therewith, and associating with the projects to the extent practicable, the persons referred to in paragraphs (b) and (c) above;

"(e) For furnishing technical publications and films;

"(f) For planning and conducting seminars;

"2. To include in the budgetary estimates of the United Nations the sums necessary for carrying out an effective operational programme based on the provision of the above services.

"B. *Instructs* the Secretary-General to undertake the performance of the functions listed in paragraph A.1 above, in agreement with the Governments concerned, on the basis of requests received from Governments and in accordance with the following policies:

"1. The kind of service to be rendered to each country shall be decided by the Government concerned;

"2. The furnishing of the experts and services shall be undertaken by the Secretary-General, with due regard to suggestions made by the requesting Governments; the Secretary-General shall, normally, make application for experts to States which are Members of the United Nations. The selection of grant holders shall be made by the Secretary-General on the basis of proposals received from Governments, which shall indicate their preferences with regard to host countries;

"3. The amount of services and the conditions under which they shall be furnished to the various Governments shall be decided by the Secretary-General with due regard to the greater needs of the under-developed areas and in conformity with the principle that each requesting Government shall be expected to assume responsibility, as far as possible, for all or part of the expenses connected with the services furnished to it, either by making a contribution in cash, or in the form of services for the purposes of the programme being carried out;

"C. *Requests* the Secretary-General to report regularly to the Social Commission on the measures which he takes in compliance with the terms of the present resolution, and requests the Commission to formulate recommendations from time to time concerning the continued action required to carry on the essential advisory activities in the field of social welfare."

5. MIGRATION AND ECONOMIC DEVELOPMENT: 624 (VII)[1]

The General Assembly,

Considering that the under-developed countries vary considerably in density of population,

Considering that in many of these and other countries, owing to the insufficiency of suitable land and of opportunities of employment, over-population is reflected in unemployment, under-employment, poverty and under-consumption.

Considering further that, in many countries with vast areas of cultivable land, sparseness of population and inadequacy of capital have been factors retarding economic development,

Noting that the Director-General of the International Labour Office in his reports to the Economic and Social Council deals with the International Labour Organisation's proposal for further action regarding methods of assisting European migration,

1. *Recommends* Member States and non-member States, classified variously as countries of emigration and of immigration, to conclude bilateral or multilateral agreements with a view to the equipment, transfer and resettlement of groups of emigrants, without racial or religious discrimination, as a part of their general economic development;

2. *Requests* the Secretary-General, the specialized agencies, in particular the International Bank for Reconstruction and Development, and other interested international organizations to continue their active cooperation in the equipment, transfer and technical training of groups of emigrants in the countries of emigration or immigration or both, by rendering such economic, financial or administrative assistance as is consistent with their respective constitutional provisions.

6. LAND REFORM: 625 (VII)[2]

. . .

B

The General Assembly,

Recalling its resolutions 401 (V) and 524 (VI) of 20 November 1950 and 12 January 1952 respectively and Economic and Social Council resolution 370 (XIII) of 7 September 1951 on land reform in underdeveloped countries,

---

[1]Adopted by 36 votes to none, with 24 abstentions, 21 December 1952.

[2]Adopted by 56 votes to none, 21 December 1952.

Taking note of the resolutions on land reform adopted by the Sixth Conference of the Food and Agriculture Organization of the United Nations,

Considering:

(a) That world food resources have increased less rapidly than world population so that in the world as a whole food consumption *per capita* is now less than it was fifteen years ago,

(b) That the lack of land and the defective agrarian structure in several geographical areas of the world are among the factors preventing a rapid increase in agricultural production in those areas and that these factors consequently render more difficult attempts to overcome food crises and to raise the general standard of living, especially in the under-developed countries,

Convinced:

(a) That the expediting of the process of bringing new lands under cultivation and the rapid improvement of the agrarian structure and present land tenure systems raise serious technical or financial problems in several geographical areas,

(b) That the isolated efforts of States Members of the United Nations to increase agricultural productivity and to bring new lands under cultivation would be more effective if they co-operated earnestly on a regional plane and if they took full advantage of available technical and financial assistance on the international plane,

(c) That the Governments of Member States and the specialized agencies should, in accordance with the recommendations contained in Economic and Social Council resolution 451 A (XIV) of 28 July 1952, make greater efforts, on the national and international plane, to grant high priority to the production and distribution of food in order to ensure a more rapid increase in the availability thereof and, by so doing, to reduce the effects of food crises by combating other natural and technical factors which lead to smaller harvests,

1. *Recommends* that the Governments of Member States take every possible step, on the national plane and, if appropriate, on a regional plane, to expedite the carrying out of their land reform programmes and, where appropriate, to bring new lands under cultivation and to increase their agricultural productivity, especially of foodstuffs, by following the recommendations and resolutions adopted by the General Assembly and by the Economic and Social Council on those questions;

2. *Invites* the Secretary-General and the specialized agencies, in carrying out their studies and activities on the questions of land reform to place particular emphasis on:

(a) The speeding up, at the request of the interested Governments and according to the circumstances prevailing in different countries or regions, of such practical measures to encourage the promotion and the carrying out of their land reform programmes as:

The convening of international and regional conferences on the development of natural resources, especially land resources, and on land administration,

The organization of seminars on problems connected with the welfare and economic and social progress of rural populations in a country or in countries of a geographical region, and

The setting up of regional centres for training experts in the several specialized fields relating to the improvement of agricultural structures;

(b) Practical measures of technical assistance so as to increase agricultural output, especially of foodstuffs, to prevent the loss of, or decrease in, harvests of those foodstuffs and to improve production methods, increase sales and encourage equitable distribution;

. . .

7. LONG-RANGE PROGRAMME FOR COMMUNITY DEVELOPMENT: 1042 (XI)[1]

The General Assembly,

Having noted chapter VI, section I, of the report of the Economic and Social Council on the programme of concerted practical action in the social field of the United Nations and the specialized agencies,

1. *Expresses its appreciation* to the Economic and Social Council for its continuous attention to practical programmes for the integrated economic and social development of the under-developed countries;

2. *Agrees* with the emphasis placed by the Council on community development as part of the comprehensive measures taken by Governments for raising levels of living, in rural areas in particular;

3. *Observes with interest* the increasing application of community development principles and processes by national Governments in their programmes for promoting balanced growth of their countries and peoples;

4. *Requests* the Secretary-General, in drawing up the recommendations called for by Council resolution 627 (XXII) of 2 August 1956 concerning the long-range programme for the promotion of community development which the Council and the Social Commission are to prepare, in collaboration with the specialized agencies, to take into account the views expressed by representatives in the Third Committee and, in particular, to lay stress upon:

(a) The integration of social and economic measures within such a programme;

---

[1] Adopted by 61 votes to none, with no abstentions.

(b) Adequate research into all factors affecting the planning and implementation of national community development programmes;

(c) The role of community development in raising levels of production, health, education and welfare and the importance of co-ordinating national and international efforts in comprehensive community development programmes;

(d) The study of the problems arising out of the migration of rural populations to urban centres;

(e) The assistance that should be given in particular to newly constituted States in planning and organizing community development programmes and in training the personnel required for implementing such programmes;

. . .

8. DEMOGRAPHIC QUESTIONS: 1217 (XII)[1]

The General Assembly.

Considering that there is a close relationship between economic problems and population problems, especially with regard to countries which are in the process of economic development,

Bearing in mind the resolutions of the General Assembly and of the Economic and Social Council which refer to the relations existing between economic development and social change,

Recalling that international co-operation towards economic development will be more effective when more is known about the population changes that accompany such development,

1. *Invites* States Members, particularly those which are in the process of economic development, to follow as closely as possible the inter-relationships existing between economic and population changes;

2. *Invites the attention* of the Economic and Social Council and of the specialized agencies concerned to the growing importance of this question;

3. *Requests* the Secretary-General to continue to ensure the co-ordination of the activities of the United Nations in the demographic and economic fields, particularly with reference to countries which are in the process of economic development;

4. *Requests* the Economic and Social Council to include pertinent information concerning the demographic activities of the Council in the chapter on economic development of its annual report to the General Assembly.

---

[1]Adopted unanimously, 14 December 1957.

9. Declaration of the Rights of the Child: 1386 (XIV) (See under Part II above.)

10. Convention on Consent to Marriage, Minimum Age for Marriage and Registration of Marriages: (763A (XVII) (See under Part II above.)

11. Population Growth and Economic Development: 1838 (XVII)[1]

The General Assembly,

Considering that rapid economic and social progress in the developing countries is dependent not least upon the ability of these countries to provide their peoples with education, a fair standard of living and the possibility for productive work,

Considering further that economic development and population growth are closely interrelated,

Recognizing that the health and welfare of the family are of paramount importance, not only for obvious humanitarian reasons, but also with regard to economic development and social progress, and that the health and welfare of the family require special attention in areas with a relatively high rate of population growth,

Recognizing further that it is the responsibility of each Government to decide on its own policies and devise its own programmes of action for dealing with the problems of population and economic and social progress,

Reminding States Members of the United Nations and members of the specialized agencies that, according to recent census results, the effective population increase during the last decade has been particularly great,

Reminding Member States that in formulating their economic and social policies it is useful to take into account the latest relevant facts on the interrelationship of population growth and economic and social development, and that the forthcoming World Population Conference and the Asian Population Conference might throw new light on the importance of this problem, especially for the developing countries,

Recalling its resolution 1217 (XII) of 14 December 1957, in which the General Assembly, *inter alia,* invited Member States, particularly the developing countries, to follow as closely as possible the interrelationship of economic changes and population changes, and requested the Secretary-General to ensure the coordination of the activities of the United Nations in the demographic and economic fields,

---

[1] Adopted by 69 votes to none, with 27 abstentions, 18 December 1962.

Recalling Economic and Social Council resolution 820 B (XXXI) of 28 April 1961 which contains provisions for intensifying efforts to ensure international cooperation in the evaluation, analysis and utilization of population census results and related data, particularly in the less developed countries, and in which the Council requested the Secretary-General to explore the possibilities of increasing technical assistance funds for assistance to Governments requesting it in preparing permanent programmes of demographic research,

Recognizing that further studies and research are necessary to fill the gaps in the present knowledge of the causes and consequences of demographic trends, particularly in the less developed countries,

Recognizing also that removals of large national groups to other countries may give rise to ethnic, political, emotional and economic difficulties,

1. *Notes with appreciation* the report of the Secretary-General on measures proposed for the United Nations Development Decade in which he refers, *inter alia*, to the interrelationship of population growth and economic and social development;

2. *Expresses its appreciation* of the work on population problems which has up to now been carried out under the guidance of the Population Commission;

3. *Requests* the Secretary-General to conduct an inquiry among the Governments of States Members of the United Nations and members of the specialized agencies concerning the particular problems confronting them as a result of the reciprocal action of economic development and population changes;

4. *Recommends* that the Economic and Social Council, in cooperation with the specialized agencies, the regional economic commissions and the Population Commission, and taking into account the results of the inquiry referred to in paragraph 3 above, should intensify its studies and research on the interrelationship of population growth and economic and social development, with particular reference to the needs of the developing countries for investment in health and educational facilities within the framework of their general development programmes;

5. *Further recommends* that the Economic and Social Council should report on its findings to the General Assembly not later than at its nineteenth session;

6. *Endorses* the view of the Population Commission that the United Nations should encourage and assist Governments, especially those of the less developed countries, in obtaining basic data and in carrying out essential studies of the demographic aspects, as well as other aspects, of their economic and social development problems;

7. *Recommends* that the second World Population Conference should pay special attention to the interrelationship of population growth and

economic and social development, particularly in the less developed countries, and that efforts should be made to obtain the fullest possible participation in the Conference by experts from such countries.

12. UNITED NATIONS DECLARATION ON THE ELIMINATION OF ALL FORMS OF RACIAL DISCRIMINATION: 1904 (XVII). (SEE UNDER PART II ABOVE.)

13. RECOMMENDATION ON CONSENT TO MARRIAGE, MINIMUM AGE FOR MARRIAGES AND REGISTRATION OF MARRIAGES: 2018 (XX)[1]

The General Assembly,

Recognizing that the family group should be strengthened because it is the basic unit of every society, and that men and women of full age have the right to marry and to found a family, that they are entitled to equal rights as to marriage and that marriage shall be entered into only with the free and full consent of the intending spouses, in accordance with the provision of article 16 of the Universal Declaration of Human Rights,

1. *Recommends* that, where not already provided by existing legislative or other measures, each Member State should take the necessary steps, in accordance with its constitutional processes and its traditional and religious practices, to adopt such legislative or other measures as may be appropriate to give effect to the following principles:

Principle I

(a) No marriage shall be legally entered into without the full and free consent of both parties, such consent to be expressed by them in person, after due publicity and in the presence of the authority competent to solemnize the marriage and of witnesses, as prescribed by law.

(b) Marriage by proxy shall be permitted only when the competent authorities are satisfied that each party has, before a competent authority and in such manner as may be prescribed by law, fully and freely expressed consent before witnesses and not withdrawn such consent.

Principle II

Member States shall take legislative action to specify a minimum age for marriage, which in any case shall not be less than fifteen years of age; no marriage shall be legally entered into by any person under this age, except where a competent authority has granted a dispensation as to age, for serious reasons, in the interest of the intending spouses.

---

[1]Adopted by 95 votes to none, with 2 abstentions, 1 November 1965.

Principle III

All marriages shall be registered in an appropriate official register by the competent authority.

14. INTERNATIONAL CONVENTION ON THE ELIMINATION OF ALL FORMS OF RACIAL DISCRIMINATION: 2106 A (XX). (SEE UNDER PART II ABOVE.)

15. INTERNATIONAL COVENANTS ON ECONOMIC, SOCIAL AND CULTURAL RIGHTS AND ON CIVIL AND POLITICAL RIGHTS: 200 A (XXI). (SEE UNDER PART II ABOVE.)

16. POPULATION GROWTH AND ECONOMIC DEVELOPMENT: 2211 (XXI)[1]

The General Assembly,

. . .

Recalling the inquiry conducted by the Secretary-General among Governments on problems resulting from the interaction of economic growth and population change, and his report thereon, which reflected a wide variety of population problems,

Commending the Economic and Social Council and the Secretary-General for convening the World Population Conference, held at Belgrade from 30 August to 10 September 1965, in which a large number of specialists in demography and related fields from developing countries were able to participate,

Taking note of the summary of the highlights of the World Population Conference,

Noting the steps taken by the organizations of the United Nations system concerned with these questions to coordinate their work in the field of population,

Concerned at the growing food shortage in the developing countries, which is due in many cases to a decline in the production of food-stuffs relative to population growth,

Recognizing the need for further study of the implications of the growth, structure and geographical distribution of population for economic and social development, including national health, nutrition, education and social welfare programmes carried out at all levels of government activity,

Believing that demographic problems require the consideration of economic, social, cultural, psychological and health factors in their proper perspective,

---

[1]Adopted unanimously, 17 December 1966.

Recognizing the sovereignty of nations in formulating and promoting their own population policies, with due regard to the principle that the size of the family should be the free choice of each individual family,

1. *Invites* the Economic and Social Council, the Population Commission, the regional economic commissions, the United Nations Economic and Social Office in Beirut and the specialized agencies concerned to study the proceedings of the 1965 World Population Conference when pursuing their activities in the field of population;

2. *Notes with satisfaction* the decision of the World Health Organization to include in its programme of activities the study of the health aspects of human reproduction and the provision of advisory services, upon request, within its responsibilities under World Health Assembly resolution WHA 19.43, and the decision of the United Nations Educational, Scientific and Cultural Organization to stimulate and provide assistance towards scientific studies concerning the relations between the development of education and population;

3. *Requests the Secretary-General:*

(a) To pursue, within the limits of available resources, the implementation of the work programme covering training, research, information and advisory services in the field of population in the light of the recommendations of the Population Commission contained in the report on its thirteenth session, as endorsed by the Economic and Social Council in its resolution 1084 (XXXIX), and of the considerations set forth in the preamble of the present resolution;

(b) To continue his consultations with the specialized agencies concerned, in order to ensure that the activities of the United Nations system of organizations in the field of population are effectively coordinated;

(c) To present to the Population Commission at its fourteenth session, as envisaged in Economic and Social Council resolution 1084 (XXXIX), proposals with regard to the priorities of work over periods of two and five years, within the framework of the long-range programme of work in the field of population;

4. *Calls upon* the Economic and Social Council, the Population Commission, the regional economic commissions, the United Nations Economic and Social Office in Beirut and the specialized agencies concerned to assist, when requested, in further developing and strengthening national and regional facilities for training, research, information and advisory services in the field of population, bearing in mind the different character of population problems in each country and region and the needs arising therefrom.

17. Declaration on the Elimination of Discrimination against Women: 2263 (XXIV). (See under Part II above.)

18. DECLARATION ON SOCIAL PROGRESS AND DEVELOPMENT: 2542 (XXIV). (SEE UNDER PART II ABOVE.)

19. INTERNATIONAL DEVELOPMENT STRATEGY FOR THE SECOND UNITED NATIONS DEVELOPMENT DECADE: 2626 (XXV). (SEE UNDER PART II ABOVE.)

20. WORLD POPULATION YEAR: 2683 (XXV)[1]

The General Assembly,

. . .

Noting also that the International Development Strategy for the Second United Nations Development Decade provides for action, both at the national and international levels, to deal with the problem of population growth in those countries which, in accordance with their concept of development, consider that their role of population growth hampers their development,

Taking into account the progress made by Member States in coping with those aspects of the population problem which are relevant to their respective economic, social, humanistic and cultural development,

Recognizing that, in spite of the progress made so far in this regard by Member States and international organizations, and particularly the important role being played in the population field by the United Nations Fund for Population Activities, varied aspects of the population problem require further attention from Member States and international organizations,

Recognizing further that a way of focusing international attention on different aspects of the population problem would be for Member States and international organizations to devote the year 1974 especially to appropriate efforts and undertakings in the field of population in the context of their respective needs and areas of competence,

Confident that the designation of the year 1974 for encouraging appropriate and relevant cooperative activity in the field of population would make a significant contribution to the realization of the objectives in this field,

1. *Designates* the year 1974 as World Population Year;

2. *Acknowledges* that the formulation and implementation of population policies and programmes are matters falling under the internal competence of each country and, consequently, that international action in the population sphere should be responsive to the varied needs and requests of individual Member States;

---

[1]Adopted by 71 votes to 8, with 31 abstentions, 11 December 1970.

3. *Requests* the Secretary-General to prepare, in consultation with interested Member States, a detailed programme of proposed measures and activities to be undertaken by the organizations of the United Nations system during the year 1974, taking into account the different character of population problems in each country and region, the population policies of Member States, as well as the proposals contained in the Secretary-General's report on the question of holding a Third World Population Conference, and to submit the programme to the Economic and Social Council in 1972 through the Population Commission at its sixteenth session;

4. *Invites* interested organizations of the United Nations system to render the necessary assistance to the Secretary-General in preparing the programme of measures and activities for the World Population Year;

5. *Invites* Member States to participate fully in the World Population Year in the context of their capacities and policies;

6. *Stresses* that assistance from organizations of the United Nations system and interested Member States should continue to be available upon request for evolving and implementing a dynamic population policy to cope with all the problems emanating from different population levels, characteristics and trends, including assistance in developing a comprehensive demographic research and studies programme as well as training programmes and in providing advisory services in this field;

7. *Requests* the Secretary-General to prepare and submit to the General Assembly in 1975, through the Economic and Social Council, a final report on the World Population Year.

21. Programme of Concerted International Action for the Advancement of Women: 2716 (XXV)[1]

The General Assembly,

. . .

Believing that a programme of concerted international action, planned on a long-term basis, will advance the status of women and increase their effective participation in all sectors,

Considering that the success of such a programme will require intensified action on the part of Member States, at the national and regional levels, as well as maximum use of the methods and techniques available through the United Nations system of organizations,

Believing that an important step in the further development of such a programme would be the establishment of concrete objectives and minimum targets,

[1]Adopted by 114 votes to none, with no abstentions, 15 December 1970.

1. *Recommends* that the objectives and targets set forth in the annex to the present resolution should be achieved as widely as possible during the Second United Nations Development Decade;

2. *Invites* States Members of the United Nations or members of specialized agencies and all organs and agencies within the United Nations system to cooperate in achieving these objectives and targets, and hopes that adequate staff and resources will be made available for this purpose;

3. *Recommends* that concerted efforts should be made to increase the resources available for technical cooperation projects which advance the status of women and that consideration be given to allocating a specific percentage of the available funds for this purpose;

. . .

ANNEX

I. GENERAL OBJECTIVES

. . .

4. The development of effective large-scale educational and informational programmes using all mass media and other available means to make all sectors of the population in rural as well as urban areas fully aware of the norms established by the United Nations and the specialized agencies in the conventions, recommendations, declarations and resolutions adopted under their auspices, and to educate public opinion and enlist its support for all measures aimed at achieving the realization of the standards set forth.

5. The assessment and evaluation of the contribution of women to the various economic and social sectors in relation to the country's over-all development plans and programmes, with a view to establishing specific objectives and minimum targets which might realistically be achieved by 1980 to increase the effective contribution of women to the various sectors.

6. The study of the positive and negative effects of scientific and technological change on the status of women with a view to ensuring continuous progress, especially as regards the education and training as well as the living conditions and employment of women.

7. The elaboration of short-term and long-term programmes to achieve these specific objectives and minimum targets, where possible within the framework of over-all national development plans or programmes, and the provision of adequate funds for programmes which advance the status of women.

8. The establishment of machinery and procedures to make possible the continuous review and evaluation of women's integration into all sectors of economic and social life and their contribution to development.

9. The full utilization of the desire and readiness of women to devote their energies, talents and abilities to the benefit of society.

II. Minimum Targets to Be Achieved During the Second United Nations Development Decade

. . .

C. Health and maternity protection

1. The progressive extension of measures to ensure maternity protection, with a view to ensuring paid maternity leave with the guarantee of returning to former or equivalent employment.

2. The development and extension of adequate child care and other facilities to assist parents with family responsibilities.

3. The adoption of measures for the creation and development of a wide network of special medical establishments for the protection of the health of the mother and child.

4. Making available to all persons who so desire the necessary information and advice to enable them to decide freely and responsibly on the number and spacing of their children and to prepare them for responsible parenthood, including information on the ways in which women can benefit from family planning. Such information and advice should be based on valid and proven scientific expertise, with due regard to the risks that may be involved.

. . .

22. Youth, its Problems and Needs, and its Participation in Social Development: 2770 (XXVI)[1]

The General Assembly,

Recognizing the important role of youth in the realization of the purposes of the Charter of the United Nations, in particular those concerning the promotion of higher standards of living and conditions of economic and social progress and development,

Emphasizing the tasks and responsibilities young people have been increasingly assuming in social and economic development, the promotion of human rights and the achievement of world peace, justice and progress,

Noting that serious problems still exist for the individual and social needs of many of the world's youth, in particular with regard to health, education, training, employment, housing and social services, and their opportunities to participate in national development, as indicated in the *1970 Report on the World Social Situation,*

Aware of the need to increase the contribution of the United Nations and the specialized agencies concerned to the education of youth, in the

---

[1]Adopted by 91 votes to none, with no abstentions, 22 November 1971.

spirit of peace, mutual understanding, friendly relations and co-operation among peoples, social justice, the dignity and value of the human person and respect for human rights and fundamental freedoms, as well as the need to enlarge their programmes and projects related to youth,

Noting that an analytical study in depth of the world social situation of youth, prepared in accordance with Economic and Social Council resolution 1407 (XLVI) of 5 June 1969, will be completed in 1972.

Bearing in mind that a report of the Secretary-General on measures to be taken to establish channels of communication with youth and international youth organizations, requested by the General Assembly in resolution 2497 (XXIV) of 28 October 1969, will be completed in 1972,

Desiring the realization of the aims of its resolution 2633 (XXV) of 11 November 1970,

Recalling paragraph 16 of that resolution, in which the General Assembly decided to resume in the future the consideration of the item entitled "Youth, its education in the respect for human rights and fundamental freedoms, its problems and needs, and its participation in national development,"

. . .

2. *Decides* to consider as soon as possible, but not later than at its twenty-eighth session, the item entitled "Youth, its education in the respect for human rights and fundamental freedoms, its problems and needs, and its active participation in national development and international co-operation."

23. WORLD SOCIAL SITUATION: 2771 (XXVI)[1]

The General Assembly,
. . .

Deeply concerned that the world social situation has continued to deteriorate, that the persistence of poverty, unemployment, hunger, disease, illiteracy, inadequate housing and uncontrolled growth of population in certain parts of the world has acquired new dimensions and that many causes of the growing disparities between the developed and developing countries hinder the advancement of the developing countries,
. . .

8. *Draws the attention* of all States and the United Nations bodies and specialized agencies concerned to the following conclusions and recommendations based upon the consideration of the *1970 Report on the World Social Situation:*
. . .

---

[1]Adopted by 95 votes to none, with 3 abstentions, 6 December 1971.

(c) Economic growth has generally been accompanied by a considerable widening of disparities in the distribution of income, wealth and services. Effective measures for promoting economic growth with social justice should receive the highest priority. Social progress will depend, to a very large extent, upon the early and vigorous implementation of a wide range of structural and institutional reforms, such as agrarian reforms, reforms aimed at securing just distribution of national wealth and income, and such programmes as measures for family planning aimed at controlling the rate of population growth in countries which consider that that rate hampers their development.

. . .

(e) The implementation of the International Development Strategy in all its interrelated aspects is an obligation of both developed and developing countries. A substantial improvement in the level of living of the masses in developing countries should be a central objective of the Second United Nations Development Decade. Improvement in the quality and distribution of social services, particularly in the fields of education, health, agriculture, housing, social welfare and social defence, should be recognized as an integral part of the over-all development effort.

. . .

(i) Broad popular participation, not only in the implementation of development programmes but also in the formulation of policies and plans and other forms of decision-making, should be regarded as both an objective and a means of development.

(j) Due attention should be paid to the needs and aspirations of the younger generation. Effective policy measures designed to involve fully the younger generation in the promotion of social progress and development should be undertaken.

(k) Adequate measures should be taken to remove discriminatory practices against women in all spheres. Greater attention should be paid to women's education, vocational training and guidance so as to ensure their full integration and participation in all aspects of economic and social life.

(l) Adequate attention should be given to multidisciplinary community services in the field of family and child welfare, particularly in situations of rapid urbanization and social change affecting family levels of living and especially the welfare of pre-school children.

. . .

24. QUESTION OF THE ELDERLY AND THE AGED: 2842 (XXVI)[1]

---

[1]Adopted unanimously, 18 December 1971.

The General Assembly,

Recalling its resolution 2599 (XXIV) of 16 December 1969 and its decision of 15 December 1970 recommending that a high priority be given to the question of the elderly and the aged,

Taking note with appreciation of the preliminary report of the Secretary-General, which reviews the major socio-economic problems of the elderly and the aged and the impact of technological and scientific advances on their well-being,

Bearing in mind the principles embodied in the Charter of the United Nations and in the Universal Declaration of Human Rights, with reference to respect for the dignity and worth of the human person,

Recalling the Declaration on Social Progress and Development, which emphasizes the protection of the rights and the assuring of the welfare of the aged,

Bearing in mind that demographic projections and anticipated social change indicate that the position of the elderly and the aged in society is expected to deteriorate in many industrialized as well as in many developing countries unless appropriate policies are initiated to deal with their needs and to ensure opportunities for their participation in national life and their contribution to the development of their communities,

Considering that the interaction of social, cultural, economic and technological factors affecting the elderly and the aged calls for integrated policies and appropriate programmes at the country level,

Noting that an exploratory cross-national survey is being conducted by the Secretary-General, in cooperation with several countries, to analyze the changing socio-economic role and status of old people,

Bearing in mind the importance for the elderly and the aged to be informed of the interest and concern of the United Nations about their welfare and needs,

1. *Requests* the Secretary-General to continue the study of the changing socio-economic and cultural role and status of the aged in countries of different levels of development and to prepare, within existing resources and in cooperation with the International Labour Organisation, the World Health Organization and other interested specialized agencies, a report suggesting guidelines for national policies and international action related to the needs and the role of the elderly and the aged in society in the context of over-all development, particularly in countries where the socio-economic problems of the aged are marked;

2. *Requests* Governments to disseminate, in the best way they deem appropriate, the information contained in the present resolution for the benefit of the elderly and the aged;

3. *Further requests* the Secretary-General to submit a report on this subject to the Economic and Social Council in 1973, through the Com-

mission for Social Development, and to report to the General Assembly at its twenty-eighth session on the action taken on the present resolution.

PART IV.

ECONOMIC AND SOCIAL COUNCIL

PART IV.
ECONOMIC AND SOCIAL COUNCIL

A. COUNCIL RESOLUTIONS

1. EMPLOYMENT: 104 (VI)[1]

The Economic and Social Council,

Taking note of the resolution unanimously adopted by the United Nations Conference on Trade and Employment on 4 February 1948,

Endorses the opinion of the Conference to the effect that the studies which have been initiated dealing with the achievement and maintenance of full and productive employment should be advanced as rapidly as possible, and that attention should be given now to methods of ensuring that high levels of employment and economic activity shall be maintained even when special factors of temporary duration now prevailing in many countries have ceased to operate,

Bearing in mind that, by virtue of its terms of reference and of the Council's resolution 26 (IV) of 28 March 1947, the Economic and Employment Commission is empowered to study problems relating to full employment,

Requests the Economic and Employment Commission to expedite the studies provided for in paragraph (c) of resolution 26 (IV) of 28 March 1947, taking into account the passage in the Conference's resolution dealing with these problems,

Requests the Secretary-General:

(a) To arrange with Members of the United Nations and, where practicable, with non-members, for the submission of information concerning action they are now taking to achieve or maintain full employment and economic stability and concerning any publicly available plans to prevent a future decline;

(b) To arrange with the appropriate specialized agencies for reports on plans which they have prepared and resources they will have available to assist members of the agency to prevent a decline in employment and economic activity; and

(c) To prepare as soon as practicable an analytical report based on the information received;

Bearing in mind that, by its resolution 42 (IV) of 29 March 1947, it instructed the Population and Social Commissions to prepare a practical plan for allocation of functions without duplication of work among the various organs concerned in the field of migration, and that by its

[1]Adopted by 15 votes to none, with 2 abstentions, 3 March 1948.

resolution 85 (V) of 13 August 1947 it transmitted for study to the International Labour Organisation a memorandum relating to the protection of migrant and immigrant labour and called the attention of the Social and Population Commissions to this memorandum,

Transmits to the International Labour Organisation, the Social Commission and the Population Commission, sections 3 and 4 of the Havana Conference's resolution dealing with population and migration problems, and

Invites them to take these sections into account in the action they are taking on those aspects of population and migration which fall in their respective fields.

2. MIGRATION: 156 (VII)[1]

A.

ALLOCATION OF FUNCTIONS

The Economic and Social Council,

Having considered the report and recommendations of the Population Commission and the Social Commission outlining their proposals for a practical plan for allocation of functions, without duplication of work, among the various organs concerned in the field of migration, submitted in accordance with the Council's resolutions of 29 March 1947, 13 August 1947 and 3 March 1948, and

Taking into account the Secretary-General's report on that question,

1. *Notes* that the Secretary-General has consulted the relevant specialized agencies on the respective functions of these agencies in the field of migration and on their interests in this field;

2. *Notes* with satisfaction the working arrangement concluded between the Secretary-General and the Director-General of the International Labour Office on their respective responsibilities in matters of migration;

3. *Endorses* the opinion of the Social Commission that the conclusion of the above working arrangement provides a favourable opportunity to define responsibility for the various matters of migration among the various organs of the Council;

4. *Notes* the opinion of the Social Commission that migration includes aspects beyond those covered in the arrangement between the Secretary-General and the Director-General of the International Labour Office and that the problem of migration is broader than the labour problem, which is only one aspect of it;

5. *Notes* that the problem of refugees and displaced persons must be distinguished from the general question of migration as a special ques-

---

[1]Adopted by 14 votes to 2, with 2 abstentions, 10 August 1948.

tion which is to be settled separately in connexion with General Assembly resolution 136 (II);

6. *Notes* that, for the solution of questions of common interest, it is desirable for the economic and social aspects of migration involving Trust Territories to be considered jointly by the Economic and Social Council and the Trusteeship Council;

7. *Decides* that the Population Commission shall arrange for studies and advise the Council on the demographic aspects of migration, on the relationships between demographic, economic and social factors in migration and on the overall co-ordination of international research and study in this field by the United Nations and the specialized agencies. These studies shall cover the trends, causes and consequences of migration and shall take into account in this connexion the influence of economic and social factors, legislative and administrative measures, the social and economic conditions of migrants, and such other factors as are important determinants in or consequences of migration;

8. *Resolves* that the Social Commission's responsibilities in this field are to arrange for studies and advise the Council on the social aspects of migration with a view, particularly, to ensuring to the migrants equal social and economic rights with those of local populations, such studies and advice to have reference especially to the following topics:

(a) The social position, rights and benefits of immigrants, including their rights and benefits when they happen to be indigent;

(b) Family and community relationships of immigrants;

(c) Advance planning by Government authorities with a view to the provision of social services and facilities for health and education, which are necessary for immigrants and their families arriving in a new community;

9. *Recalls* that, in addition to the Population and Social Commissions, all the other functional commissions of the Council may have to deal with aspects of migration which fall within their respective assignments, the co-ordination of the activities of the commissions being the task of the Council;

10. *Invites* the regional economic commissions and the functional commissions of the Council to consult together, when desirable, through the Secretary-General, on migration problems which may be put to them, and to keep the Population and Social Commissions informed of such consultations;

11. *Requests* the Secretary-General to consult with those non-governmental organizations which are interested in migration problems and particularly with trade union organizations, and to seek their advice in order to ascertain whether these organizations can make arrangements for co-ordinating their respective activities;

B.
PROTECTION OF MIGRANT AND IMMIGRANT LABOUR[1]

The Economic and Social Council,

Having considered the report of the Secretary-General on the allocation of functions among the various organs concerned in the field of migration, and the report and recommendations of the Social Commission relating to migration, and taking into account the memorandum on migration submitted by the International Labour Organization in accordance with Council resolution 85 (V) of 13 August 1947,

Notes with satisfaction that the Governing Body of the International Labour Office, conscious of the importance and the urgency of the problem, has placed revision of the Migration for Employment Convention, 1939, and its related recommendations on the agenda of the thirty-second session of the International Labour Conference;

Expresses the wish that, pending the adoption and ratification of an international convention providing adequate protection of migrant and immigration labour, Member Governments, in determining their respective policies in this field, should be guided by the principle of equality of treatment in social and economic matters of national and foreign workers;

Expresses also the wish that international arrangements in matters of migration include as soon as possible:

(a) Broadening of the present system of international information in matters of migration so as to assure the immediate availability of knowledge on migration possibilities and conditions for use by government and voluntary organizations and by migrants or prospective migrants;

(b) Means for the improvement of statistics on international migration so as to increase their adequacy and comparability.

3. ECONOMIC DEVELOPMENT OF UNDER-DEVELOPED COUNTRIES:
    222 (IX)[2]

A.
EXPANDED PROGRAMME OF TECHNICAL ASSISTANCE FOR ECONOMIC DEVELOPMENT OF UNDER-DEVERLOPED COUNTRIES

Resolution of 15 August 1949

The Economic and Social Council,

Having considered the report prepared by the Secretary-General, in consultation with the specialized agencies, on an expanded programme

---

[1]Adopted by 13 votes to 2, with 3 abstentions, 10 August 1948.

[2]Adopted by 16 votes to none.

of technical assistance for economic development, pursuant to resolution 180 (VIII),

Being impressed with the significant contribution to economic development that can be made by an expansion of the international interchange of technical knowledge through international co-operation among countries,

Believing that a sound international programme of this character must combine and make use of the experience of many nations, with different social patterns and cultural traditions and at different stages of development, so as to facilitate progress in the less-advanced countries and to help solve their technical and economic problems,

3. *Requests* the Secretary-General, subject to such decision as may be taken by the General Assembly on the draft resolution in Annex II, to invite the Administrative Committee on Co-ordination to set up a Technical Assistance Board (TAB) which shall consist of the executive heads, or their representatives, of the United Nations and of the specialized agencies which participate in accordance with this paragraph in the expanded programme of technical assistance. The Secretary-General, or his representative, shall be Chairman of the Board.

. . .

(h) All decisions other than on procedural matters shall be taken by general agreement and, when agreement cannot be reached, the issue in dispute shall be referred for decision to the TAC;

4. *Authorizes* the Secretary-General, after consultation with the other participating organizations, to designate the Executive Secretary of the TAB,

. . .

6. *Decides* to establish, . . . a standing Technical Assistance Committee of the Council (TAC), consisting of the members of the Council, which is authorized to sit while the Council is not in session and which shall have the following terms of reference:

(a) To make for the Council critical examinations of activities undertaken and results achieved under the expanded programme of technical assistance;

(b) To examine each year's programme presented to it by the TAB and report to the Council concerning it, making such recommendations as it may deem necessary;

(c) To interpret this resolution in cases of conflicts or questions submitted to it by the TAB, through its Chairman, and decide any such conflicts or questions;

(d) To receive reports from the TAB on progress and implementation of, and disbursements of funds under the expanded programme;

(e) To review the working relationships between the participating organizations and the effectiveness of the methods of co-ordination in connexion with their technical assistance programmes, making recommendations when appropriate;

(f) To perform such other relevant functions as the Council may assign to it from time to time;

. . .

12. *Decides*, subject to such decision as may be taken by the General Assembly on the draft resolution in Annex II, to call, in accordance with the supplementary rule of procedure of the General Assembly on the calling of international conferences by the Economic and Social Council, a Technical Assistance Conference for the purpose of:

(a) Ascertaining the total amount of contributions available from participating Governments for the execution of the technical assistance programme of the United Nations and the specialized agencies during the first year of its operation;

. . .

4. REPORT OF THE POPULATION COMMISSION: 471 (XV)

A.[1]

The Economic and Social Council,

Taking note of the report of the Population Commission (seventh session),

Viewing with satisfaction the progress made by the Population Commission, in co-operation with the Statistical Commission, in improving the quality and availability of basic demographic information and in creating a continuing programme for further improvement of such information,

Recognizing the importance of such improvement of basic information for the full performance of the other responsibilities of the Population Commission,

Welcomes the decision of the Commission to concentrate its future efforts and resources on three major lines of work now underway, namely:

(1) Studies of the interrelationships of demographic, economic, and social factors;

(2) Analyses of future population trends; and

(3) Studies of migration, both international and internal.

B.[2]

The Economic and Social Council,

Recalling its interest in the studies of the interrelationships of demo-

---

[1]Adopted by 16 votes to none, with 2 abstentions, 14 April 1953.

[2]Adopted by 16 votes to none, with 2 abstentions.

graphic, economic and social factors being carried forward by the Secretary-General (resolution 308 D (XI)),

Noting the summary of the major study conducted by the Secretary-General entitled "Determinants and Consequences of Population Trends", to which the Population Commission drew its attention,

Draws the attention of Member States to the importance of obtaining fuller information on, and of considering the interrelationships between, population changes and economic and social changes in developing various portions of their economic and social programmes aimed at raising the standard of living of their peoples.

C.[1]

The Economic and Social Council,

Having in mind the great potential value of the results of the population censuses taken in various countries during recent years as a basis for analytical studies which would elucidate major social and economic problems facing Member States,

1. *Invites* the Governments of those countries and territories where population censuses have recently been taken, or will be taken in the near future, to prepare analytical studies based on either complete or sample tabulations of census results, devoting primary attention to those demographic topics which are of foremost importance to their programmes of economic and social development and taking into account, in the selection of topics, the views on this matter expressed by the Population Commission at its seventh session;

2. *Requests* the Secretary-General to give, within the limits of the resources available and in accordance with the work priorities, appropriate technical assistance to those Governments requesting aid in order to help them carry out analytical studies of their census results.

D.[2]

The Economic and Social Council,

Considering the importance of internal migration in connexion with economic progress and the attendant social and political phenomena, especially in the economically under-developed countries, and noting that in these countries internal migration has not been sufficiently studied, and

Paying due attention to the priorities established for the implementation of the work programme of the Population Commission,

1. *Recommends* that Member States continue to give special atten-

---

[1]Adopted by 16 votes to none, with 2 abstentions.
[2]Adopted by 15 votes to 2, with 1 abstention.

tion to the problem of internal migration and its social and economic implications, particularly within a process of economic development;

2. *Invites* Member States to take appropriate action with a view to improving the statistical and demographic information in the field of internal migration;

3. *Recommends* that the Secretary-General, in co-operation with the appropriate specialized agencies, aid those Member States requesting technical assistance pertaining to the field of internal migration;

4. *Calls the attention* of Member States having similar problems relating to internal migration to the advantage of conducting joint studies, and further directs the attention of the regional economic commissions to the importance of internal migration especially in connexion with economic development.

. . .

5. POPULATION QUESTIONS: 571 (XIX)[1]
. . .
B.

The Economic and Social Council,

Having considered the report of the Population Commission on the proposal of the Secretary-General to arrange for a part of the programme of population studies to be carried out by universities and other outside scientific institutions in co-operation with the Secretariat,

1. *Emphasizes* the need to maintain an adequate programme of studies on population trends and their relation to economic and social factors, especially in the development of the less developed countries;

2. *Requests* the Secretary-General:

(a) To make an effort to obtain the co-operation of qualified scientific institutions in those parts of the programme of population studies in which such co-operation would be most useful, on the largest scale that is feasible in view of the available financial and other resources, with adequate safeguards to ensure the maintenance of a high standard of quality and objectivity in the work done by outside scientific institutions on behalf of the United Nations;

(b) To give considerations, in selecting the scientific institutions to be invited to co-operate in portions of the programme, to the importance of an adequate distribution, particularly from a geographical point of view, and to the need for expanding the capacity of existing scientific institutions in certain countries, notably in the less developed regions, for research on the problems of population;

(c) To explore the possibility of establishing standing co-operative relations with qualified scientific institutions in each of the major under-

---

[1]Adopted unanimously, 27 May 1955.

developed regions of the world, which could serve as centres for studies on population problems of importance in the region and for the training of personnel in this field of study on a regional basis;

(d) To explore the possibilities of co-operation in the programme of regional centres of demographic study and training, on the part of scientific institutions in other regions which have highly developed facilities for work in this field, and on the part of non-governmental organizations and private foundations;

3. *Recommends* that Governments, especially of the less developed countries which have expressed the desire to conduct population studies in their countries in accordance with the Population Commission's programme, should (a) consider the possibilities of facilitating co-operation between the Secretariat and qualified scientific institutions in the countries concerned in carrying out portions of the programme of population studies, and (b) give attention in this connexion to possible technical assistance projects for training needed personnel and for aid in the planning and direction of study projects.

C.

The Economic and Social Council,

Having in mind the importance of the questions discussed at the World Population Conference for governmental policies and action programmes, particularly for the economic and social development of the under-developed countries and for the programmes of regional economic commissions,

Recalling the interest aroused by the work of the Secretariat on the interrelationships of demographic, economic and social factors published under the title *The Determinants and Consequences of Population Trends,*

1. *Invites* interested Governments, specialized agencies, regional economic commissions and non-governmental organizations to examine the proceedings of the Conference and the work of the Secretariat in the field of population and to give due consideration to demographic factors in programmes of action in the economic and social fields;

2. *Suggests* to Governments that one way to facilitate this examination would be to create national committees composed of the representatives of interested governmental agencies and institutions, as well as individual experts in the different scientific disciplines concerned, for the purpose of giving advice on the relevance on population studies to policies and action programmes and on further investigations that may be desirable;

. . .

6. REPORT OF THE POPULATION COMMISSION: 642 (XXIII)[1]

. . .

B.

The Economic and Social Council,

Recognizing that there is a direct relationship between the problems of population and economic and social development,

Considering that after the establishment of demographic training and research centres in Latin America and in Asia and the Far East, the time has come to focus attention on demographic problems in Africa,

Considering further that the existence of new States in Africa justifies increased attention to these problems,

. . .

Considering the desirability of making as much preparation as possible for deriving maximum results from the forthcoming population censuses in Africa,

Requests the Secretary-General, in consultation with the Governments concerned, specialized agencies and other appropriate international agencies, to study the possibilities of encouraging wider co-operation in demographic studies and in the improvement of census and vital statistics in Africa and explore the desirability and feasibility of the early establishment of demographic training and research centres in Africa, and to report as appropriate to the Population Commission at its tenth session.

C.

The Economic and Social Council,

Recognizing the importance of technical assistance in the demographic field for the economic and social development of under-developed countries,

Recalling the request made to the Secretary-General, in Council resolution 471 C (XV) of 14 April 1953, to give, within the limits of the resources available and in accordance with the work priorities, appropriate technical assistance to those Governments requesting aid in order to help them carry out analytical studies of their census results,

Considering the small number of experts available in this field in most countries and the difficulties which have been experienced in recruiting qualified experts for demographic missions,

1. *Recommends* that Governments interested in obtaining technical assistance in the demographic field make their requests as early as possible;

---

[1]Adopted 25 April 1957.

2. *Urges* Governments to assist the United Nations in its efforts to recruit demographic experts for technical assistance missions by making such experts available to the greatest extent possible;

3. *Invites* the specialized agencies, particularly the United Nations Educational, Scientific and Cultural Organization, to collaborate with the United Nations in this field, in view of their contacts with non-governmental organizations and institutions which have consultative status or maintain relations with these specialized agencies.

7. REPORT OF THE POPULATION COMMISSION (TENTH SESSION): 721 (XXVII)[1]

. . .

B.
DEMOGRAPHIC PILOT STUDIES

The Economic and Social Council,

Taking note of the section of the report of the Population Commission (tenth session) on demographic pilot studies,

Reaffirming that it is essential to take demographic factors into account in planning economic and social development programmes, particularly in under-developed countries,

Recalling the importance attached by the Council to surveys of human and material resources and needs, with a view to facilitating the planning of economic development programmes for the under-developed countries, in accordance with its resolution 614 C (XXII) of August 1956,

Bearing in mind the fact that many countries will be carrying out population censuses during 1960 and 1961, and the importance of utilizing the results of these censuses to facilitate the planning of development programmes for the under-developed countries, as well as for other purposes,

Requests the Secretary-General:

(a) To take the necessary steps, as soon as possible, to publish a report on the demographic pilot study carried out in co-operation with the Government of the Philippines;

(b) To put at the disposal of the Governments of under-developed countries which may request it the co-operation of the United Nations in carrying out, over the next few years, a limited number of demographic pilot studies or other projects calculated to demonstrate the value of utilizing demographic data, and especially the results of censuses, in preparing and implementing development programmes; such

---

[1]Adopted unanimously 24 April 1959.

studies, carried out in accordance with the recommendations of the Population Commission, would also enable the methods of obtaining the data to be made known and perfected;

(c) To obtain, in so far as this is desirable and feasible, the collaboration in such projects of the specialized agencies and other bodies concerned;

C.
DEMOGRAPHIC ASPECTS OF URBANIZATION AND INDUSTRIALIZATION WITH SPECIAL REFERENCE TO THE STUDY OF INTERNAL MIGRATION

The Economic and Social Council,

Taking note of the section of the report of the Population Commission (tenth session) on possibilities of international co-operation in studies of internal migration in the less developed countries in the process of industrialization,

Recognizing the importance of studies of internal migration in relation to economic and social development, especially in the countries in the process of industrialization,

Recalling that, in its resolutions 618 (XXII) of 6 August 1956 and 694 C (XXVI) of 31 July 1958, it had requested the Secretary-General to explore the possibilities of concerting international action in connexion with problems of urbanization which should complement the programmes of industrialization,

Considering the lack of knowledge and the inadequacy of reliable data with which to measure the phenomena of rural to urban migration and the contrary movement,

Requests the Secretary-General to develop studies of internal migration in relation to economic and social development, along the following lines:

(a) To offer the co-operation of the United Nations to less developed countries in the process of industrialization which are desirous of undertaking studies of the magnitude and characteristics of internal migration, especially between rural and urban areas, as a part of the programme of demographic studies recommended by the Population Commission;

(b) In the development of these studies to take account of relevant social and economic changes associated with the processes of urbanization and industrialization, by observing conditions at first hand and with the co-operation of local organizations;

(c) To invite the co-operation of the interested specialized agencies in this work as a part of the proposed programmes of concerted action in the fields of urbanization and industrialization;

(d) To report to the Population Commission at its eleventh session on the progress made in implementing these requests.

8. Report of the Population Commission: 820 (XXXI)[1]

. . .

B.

1960 World Population Census Programme

The Economic and Social Council,

Taking note of that part of the report of the Population Commission (eleventh session) which deals with the 1960 World Population Census Programme, with special reference to the evaluation, analysis and utilization of the results of the censuses,

Having in mind the necessity of ensuring a rapid rate of growth of employment and production, particularly in economically less developed areas,

Considering that adequate information on population trends and characteristics and their interrelations with economic and social factors in each country form a necessary part of the basis for constructing sound national policies and programmes of action for developing and utilizing human resources and satisfying the needs of the people,

Emphasizing the value of the information relevant to these questions which can be obtained from appropriate studies of the results of national censuses taken in connexion with the 1960 World Population Census Programme,

1. *Invites* Governments of Member States taking part in this Programme to consider the utility of making whatever arrangements may be necessary and practicable in each country to ensure that essential analyses of the census results will be carried out, particularly as they relate to important national problems of economic and social development and to questions of national demographic, economic and social policy;

2. *Requests* the Secretary-General:

(a) To intensify, during the next few years, efforts to ensure international co-operation in the evaluation, analysis and utilization of population census results and related data, especially in less developed countries:

(i) By expanding and diversifying existing internationally sponsored facilities for demographic training and research;

(ii) By developing such facilities in regions where they do not yet exist, especially in Africa;

[1]Adopted unanimously 28 April 1961.

(iii) By making available to Governments of under-developed countries, at their request, the services of expert consultants to advise and assist in national projects of evaluation, analysis and utilization of census results and related data, and in national or sub-regional seminars for the discussion of relevant problems of research;

(iv) By assisting such Governments, at their request, to establish continuing, institutionalized programmes of demographic research in the government services or in research institutions or universities;

(b) To explore the possibilities of increasing the amounts of technical assistance funds which may be made available for activities of the types listed above, and the possibilities of obtaining supplementary funds from other sources;

. . .

9. REPORT OF THE POPULATION COMMISSION: 933 (XXXV)[1]

. . .

B.
WORLD POPULATION CONFERENCE, 1965

The Economic and Social Council,

. . .

Considering the recommendation of the General Assembly in resolution 1838 (XVII) of 18 December 1962 that the second World Population Conference should pay special attention to the interrelationships of population growth with economic and social development, particularly in the less developed countries, and that efforts should be made to obtain the fullest possible participation in the Conference by experts from such countries,

. . .

Commending the inter-agency collaboration established in the planning and organizational work preparatory to the Conference,

1. *Takes note* of the recommendations of the Preparatory Committee defining the objectives of the Conference;

2. *Requests* the Secretary-General, in connexion with his plans for financing the second World Population Conference:

(a) To lend his support to the efforts being made to obtain the fullest participation in the Conference by experts from less developed countries;

(b) To continue consultations with interested specialized agencies with a view to arranging for their fullest participation;

(c) To seek provision in his 1964, 1965 and 1966 budget estimates

---

[1]Adopted unanimously 5 April 1963.

for United Nations participation, with the hope that adequate resources will be provided by the General Assembly;

(d) To continue his efforts to obtain the maximum financial support of non-governmental organizations and foundations;

3. *Further requests* the Secretary-General:

(a) To convene the Conference during 1965;

(b) To present a recommendation to the Economic and Social Council, at its thirty-sixth session, on the site of the Conference, bearing in mind:

(i) The generous offer by the Government of Yugoslavia and the terms of General Assembly resolution 1202 (XII) of 13 December 1957 concerning the pattern of conferences;

(ii) The recommendation contained in the report of the eleventh session of the Population Commission stressing the desirability of holding the Conference in an under-developed country;

(iii) The suggestion of the Preparatory Committee that preference should be given to a country in Africa or Latin America;

(iv) The results of the further efforts that will be made to ascertain the interests and possibilities of the Governments of various countries as regards the organization of the Conference.

C.
INTENSIFICATION OF DEMOGRAPHIC STUDIES, RESEARCH AND TRAINING

The Economic and Social Council,

Taking note of General Assembly resolution 1838 (XVII) of 18 December 1962, which recommends intensified study and research on the interrelationship of population growth and social and economic development, with particular reference to the developing countries, and endorses the view of the Population Commission that the United Nations should encourage and assist developing countries in obtaining basic data and in carrying out studies of the demographic aspects of development,

Bearing in mind the report entitled *The United Nations Development Decade: Proposals for Action*, which acknowledges that the lack of basic economic and social statistics and surveys in many of the developing countries is a well-known obstacle to progress since it deprives the Governments of an adequate quantitative basis for their development plans, and bearing in mind, also, General Assembly resolution 1710 (XVI) of 19 December 1961,

Recognizing the growing contribution and the growing responsibility of the Secretary-General and of the specialized agencies to ensure that the developing countries obtain and analyse the population data required for the effective implementation of their social and economic development, and to improve the understanding of the interrelationships between population change and social and economic development,

Emphasizing the importance of supplementing the efforts of the Secretary-General and the specialized agencies in these fields by action on the part of Member States co-ordinated with those of the Secretary-General, including bilateral arrangements among the Member States,

1. *Invites* the Economic Commission for Africa, the Economic Commission for Asia and the Far East and the Economic Commission for Latin America to examine the possibilities of intensifying their work in the demographic field within the general framework of the programme recommended by the Population Commission in the report on its twelfth session and with special reference to the recommendation of the General Assembly in resolution 1838 (XVII) for intensified studies of the interrelationships of population growth and economic and social growth;

2. *Requests* the Secretary-General, in co-operation with the specialized agencies, where appropriate:

(a) To accelerate work on technical manuals on the analysis of census data, on methods of estimating fundamental demographic measures, on methods of projecting the economically active population, school enrollment, rural and urban population, and the number of households, because of their importance for the United Nations Development Decade, and the urgent necessity to make efficient use of the results of the world census programme;

(b) To hasten the completion of the revised edition of *Determinants and Consequences of Population Trends,* so that it may be used in connexion with the 1965 World Population Conference;

(c) To study the uses of electronic computers in the analysis of demographic data;

3. *Further requests* the Secretary-General to give serious consideration to the provision, both at Headquarters and at the regional level, of the necessary financial and staff resources within the limits of the available resources for the economic and social programmes for 1963 to enable the prompt execution of the programmes proposed by the Population Commission in the report on its twelfth session, and to complete the work requested in paragraph 2 above;

4. *Requests* the General Assembly to provide adequate resources to permit the continued effective execution of the programmes recommended by the Population Commission;

5. *Invites* those States Members of the United Nations and members of the specialized agencies which are developed countries to consider the value to the developing countries of initiating or expanding the following activities, in co-ordination with the activities of the Secretary-General and the specialized agencies:

(a) Research which would enhance the understanding of the relationship between population trends and social and economic development, and hence would improve economic and social planning — such research to include analysis of the historical records of population trends and social and economic change in the more developed countries — and basic research in the methods of demography, such as the measurement of fertility, mortality and migration;

(b) Research which would increase the effectiveness of social and economic programmes of studies related to population, such as research on health and education;

(c) Training of experts and technicians from the less developed countries in demography and statistics, expanding the scope of such training in universities and government agencies, and providing support for students from the less developed countries;

(d) Providing technical assistance to the developing countries in preparing, executing, tabulating and analysing population censuses, in establishing the registration of vital events, and in utilizing demographic data and analysis in social and economic planning.

10. POPULATION GROWTH AND ECONOMIC AND SOCIAL DEVELOPMENT: 1048 (XXXVII)[1]

The Economic and Social Council,

. . .

Having considered with appreciation the inquiry conducted by the Secretary-General as requested by the General Assembly among Governments of States Members of the United Nations or members of the specialized agencies concerning the particular problems confronting them as a result of the reciprocal action of economic development and population changes,

Having noted in particular the serious concern expressed in reply to the inquiry by many Governments of developing countries about the slow rate of economic growth of their countries in relation to the high rate of their population growth,

Having further noted the high priority given by the Advisory Committee on the Application of Science and Technology, *inter alia*, to "the objective of a more complete understanding of population problems",

Commending the Economic Commission for Asia and the Far East for organizing the Asian Population Conference held in 1963,

1. *Invites* the General Assembly, the regional economic commissions and the Population Commission to examine the replies of the Gov-

---

[1]Adopted unanimously 15 August 1964.

ernments to the inquiry and to make recommendations with a view to intensifying the work of the United Nations in assisting the Governments of the interested developing countries to deal with the population problems confronting them;

2. *Requests* the Secretary-General to circulate the findings of the inquiry to the World Population Conference and to the specialized agencies concerned, in particular the International Labour Organisation, the Food and Agriculture Organization, the United Nations Educational, Scientific and Cultural Organization and the World Health Organization, with the suggestion that they take the findings into account, as appropriate, in formulating their programmes;

3. *Requests* the Secretary-General to undertake in the future, at appropriate intervals, similar inquiries on problems resulting from the relationship between economic development and population changes;

4. *Draws the attention* of the General Assembly to resolution 54 (XX) unanimously adopted by the Economic Commission for Asia and the Far East on 17 March 1964 which invites "the United Nations and the specialized agencies to expand the scope of the technical assistance they are prepared to give, upon the request of Governments, in the development of statistics, research experimentation and action programmes related to population";

5. *Recommends* that the Economic Commission for Latin America and the Economic Commission for Africa organize regional conferences, study the population trends as well as the economic trends connected with them and their implications for economic and social development in the regions concerned, and to communicate their findings to the Council and to the Population Commission for appropriate action;

6. *Urges* the Secretary-General and the specialized agencies concerned to explore ways and means of strengthening and expanding their work in the field of population, including the possibilities of obtaining voluntary contributions.

11. Work Programmes and Priorities in Population Fields: 1084 (XXXIX)[1]

The Economic and Social Council,

. . .

Bearing in mind the problems in the economic and social development of developing countries associated with the growth and structure of population and migration from the countryside to cities,

Recalling the concern with these problems expressed in the responses of many Governments of developing countries to the inquiry among

---
[1]Adopted unanimously 30 July 1965.

Governments on problems resulting from the interaction of economic development and population changes carried out in accordance with the above-mentioned resolution [1838 (XVII)] of the General Assembly,

Taking note of the views expressed by the Population Commission in the report of its thirteenth session on population growth and economic and social development and on possibilities of assisting Governments of developing countries in dealing with population problems, and in particular the Population Commission's recommendations on the long-range programme of work of the United Nations and the specialized agencies in the population fields,

Being aware that many countries lack technical personnel with specialized training in population questions and facilities for training national technicians,

Considering that there is a need to intensify and extend the scope of the work of the United Nations and the specialized agencies relating to population questions,

1. *Endorses* the recommendations of the Population Commission in the report of its thirteenth session on the long-range programme of work in the fields of population, including its recommendations with regard to the increase and improvement of demographic statistics, the strengthening of regional demographic training and research centres, and other activities to increase the supply of technically trained personnel in the developing countries, expansion and intensification of research and technical work, widening of the scope and increase of the amount of technical assistance in population fields available to Governments of developing countries upon their request, and conferences and related activities in the population fields;

2. *Draws the attention* of the Statistical Commission, the Social Commission and the Commission on the Status of Women to the recommendations and suggestions of the Population Commission relating to activities in their fields of interest;

3. *Invites* the regional economic commissions and the interested specialized agencies to give consideration to possibilities of modifying and expanding their programmes of activities in the population fields along the lines indicated by the recommendations of the Population Commission;

4. *Calls to the attention* of the General Assembly the need to provide the necessary resources, within the framework of the decisions taken to balance the budget of the United Nations, for the United Nations to carry out the intensified and expanded programme of activities in the fields of population recommended by the Population Commission;

5. *Requests* the Secretary-General,

(a) To consider giving a position for the work in population in the United Nations Secretariat that would correspond to its importance;

(b) To provide, in accordance with Council resolution 222 (IX) of 14 and 15 August 1949 and General Assembly resolution 418 (V) of 1 December 1950, advisory services and training on action programmes in the field of population at the request of Governments desiring assistance in this field;

(c) To consult the interested specialized agencies on the division of responsibilities and co-ordination of activities in the long-range programme of work in the population fields recommended by the Population Commission;

(d) To present to the Population Commission at its fourteenth session proposals with regard to the priorities of work over future periods of two years and of five years, within the framework of the long-range programme of work in the population fields.

12. United Nations Development Decade: 1089 (XXXIX)[1]

The Economic and Social Council,

Reaffirming General Assembly resolution 1710 (XVI) of 19 December 1961 which designated the current decade as the United Nations Development Decade in which the developing Member States would intensify their efforts to achieve self-sustaining growth with the objective of attaining a minimum annual rate of growth of aggregate national income of 5 per cent at the end of the decade,

. . .

Recognizing that the rapid growth in population in many developing countries in relation to the growth of their national income calls for the most urgent action,

Aware that the developments in science and technology have placed in the hands of mankind the means necessary for abolishing poverty, ignorance and disease,

1. *Urges* the States Members of the United Nations or members of the specialized agencies and the International Atomic Energy Agency, and particularly the developed countries:

. . .

(e) To augment the resources for developmental activities within the United Nations family and particularly to contribute as a matter of urgency their utmost to the United Nations programmes of technical co-operation and to attain the target for the World Food Programme for the years 1966-1968;

. . .

---

[1]Adopted unanimously 31 July 1965.

13. Enlargement of Subsidiary Organs of the Council: 1147 (XLI)[1]

The Economic and Social Council,

Recalling its resolution 845 (XXXII) of 3 August 1961, in which it established the present level of membership of its functional commissions,

Noting that since its thirty-second session there has been a further increase in the membership of the United Nations,

Taking into consideration the deep interest of many States Members of the United Nations in participating in, and contributing to, the work of these subsidiary bodies of experts,

1. *Decides* to enlarge, with effect from 1 January 1967, the Commission on Human Rights, the Commission for Social Development and the Commission on the Status of Women to thirty-two members each, these members to be elected on the basis of an equitable geographical distribution according to the following pattern:

(a) Eight members from African States;

(b) Six members from Asian States;

(c) Six members from Latin American States;

(d) Eight members from western European and other States;

(e) Four members from socialist States of eastern Europe;

2. *Decides* to enlarge, with effect from 1 January 1967, the Population Commission and the Committee on Housing, Building and Planning to twenty-seven members each, to be elected on the basis of an equitable geographical distribution according to the following pattern:

(a) Seven members from African States;

(b) Five members from Asian States;

(c) Five members from Latin American States;

(d) Seven members from western European and other States;

(e) Three members from socialist States of eastern Europe;

3. *Decides* to enlarge the Statistical Commission to twenty-four members, to be elected on the basis of an equitable geographical distribution according to the following pattern:

(a) Five members from African States;

(b) Four members from Asian States;

(c) Four members from Latin American States;

(d) Seven members from western European and other States;

(e) Four members from socialist States of eastern Europe;

---

[1]Adopted unanimously 4 August 1966.

14. Principles and Recommendations for the 1970 Population and Housing Censuses: 1215 (XLII)[1]

The Economic and Social Council,

Taking note of the report of the Statistical Commission on its fourteenth session and the adoption by the Commission of principles and recommendations for population censuses and housing censuses to be taken around 1970,

Recalling General Assembly resolution 1710 (XVI) of 19 December 1961 on the United Nations Development Decade, which requested the Secretary-General to develop proposals for the intensification of action in the fields of economic and social development with particular reference to the need to review facilities for the collection, collation, analysis and dissemination of statistical and other information required for charting economic and social development and for providing a constant measurement of progress towards the objectives of the Decade.

Recognizing the important role of population censuses and housing censuses as primary sources of basic national data for achieving the above-mentioned purposes,

Further recalling its resolution 1054 B (XXXIX) of 16 July 1965, which requested the Secretary-General to proceed with the development of 1970 world population and housing census programmes and recommended that Member States undertake to carry out population and housing censuses during the period 1965-1974 and that they take into account the international recommendations in order that the censuses might meet national requirements and facilitate the study of population and housing problems on a world-wide basis,

1. *Requests* the Secretary-General to publish his reports entitled "Principles and Recommendations for a Population Census" and "Principles and Recommendations for a Housing Census", as modified, and to distribute copies to States Members of the United Nations, to States members of the specialized agencies, to appropriate regional bodies and to specialized agencies;

2. *Further requests* the Secretary-General to give assistance to Governments in the implementation of these principles and recommendations by mobilizing all available resources to help in the very large task of meeting the needs of countries in this area, and by the revision of the *Handbook of Population Census Methods*, the preparation of a handbook of housing census methods, the preparation of a technical manual on methods of evaluating population and housing census results, and the provision of technical advice and fellowships under the United Nations Development Programme.

---

[1]Adopted unanimously 1 June 1967.

114

15. Development of Activities in the Field of Population: 1279 (XLIII)[1]

The Economic and Social Council,

. . .

Having heard the statement of the Secretary-General that the United Nations can now embark on a bolder and more effective programme of action in the field of population and with the co-operation of the World Health Organization, the United Nations Children's Fund and other interested agencies, the United Nations has now at its disposal an institutional infrastructure which, given some additional means, could be put to much more effective use in support of large-scale programmes,

Noting that, in addition to previous resolutions enabling the World Health Organization to advise Governments, on request, on the health aspects of family planning as part of health services, the Twentieth World Health Assembly requested the Director-General of the World Health Organization to continue to develop the activities of the World Health Organization in the field of health aspects of human reproduction and to assist on request in national research projects and in securing the training of university teachers and of professional staff,

Noting further that the fifty-first session of the International Labour Conference requested the Director-General of the International Labour Office through the Governing Body to undertake a comprehensive study on the influence and consequences of rapid population growth on opportunities for training and employment and on welfare of workers, with particular reference to developing countries and to cooperate closely towards this aim with the United Nations and other competent international organizations,

Noting also Resolution 3.252 of the fourteenth session of the General Conference of the United Nations Educational, Scientific and Cultural Organization on the subject of education and evolution of population and the related work plan, which provides *inter alia* for a consideration of sociological studies on social, cultural, and other factors influencing attitudes for family planning, taking into consideration the economic aspects of population problems,

Urges all organizations within the United Nations system to make every effort, within their competence, with a view to developing and rendering more effective their programmes in the field of population, including training, research, information and advisory services; and in particular invites the United Nations Educational, Scientific and Cultural Organization to pursue actively its education, social sciences and mass media activities in this regard.

[1]Adopted by 19 votes to none, with 5 abstentions, 4 August 1967.

16.   Family Planning and the Status of Women: 1326 (XLIV)[1]

The Economic and Social Council,

Considering that the General Assembly in its resolution 2211 (XXI) of 17 December 1966 recognized the sovereignty of nations in formulating and promoting their own population policies, with due regard to the principle that the size of the family should be the free choice of each individual family,

Considering that the General Assembly in the Declaration on the elimination of Discrimination against Women, unanimously adopted on 7 November 1967, has recognized the equal right of men and women to access to educational information to help in ensuring the health and well-being of families,

Noting the mandate and activities of the United Nations system of organization in the population field,

Noting also that various family planning programmes offer services which include education for responsible parenthood, the treatment of sterility, the provision of maternal and child care facilities, and the dissemination of educational information, including sex education and marriage counselling,

Recognizing that such programmes as they are evolving today have important implications for women in several fields,

1. *Requests* the Secretary-General to transmit the interim report relating to the status of women and family planning to States Members of the United Nations and members of the specialized agencies, to the specialized agencies concerned, and to interested non-governmental organizations;

2. *Invites* interested Governments of States Members of the United Nations and members of the specialized agencies:

(a) To undertake national surveys or case studies on the status of women and family planning, taking into account such factors as the implication for the status of women of the effects of population growth on economic and social development, factors affecting fertility that relate directly to the status of women, the implications of family size for maternal and child welfare, the scope of existing family palnning programmes in relation to the status of women, and current trends in population growth and family size and the protection of human rights, in particular the rights of women;

(b) To make their findings available to the Secretary-General as the basis for a further report on this question;

3. *Invites* the specialized agencies concerned to cooperate within their

---

[1] Adopted by 23 votes to none, with 4 abstentions.

respective fields of competence in the further study of the relationship of the status of women and family planning;

4. *Requests* interested non-governmental organizations to make available to the Secretary-General any relevant material they may have relating to the factors mentioned in paragraph 2 (a) above;

5. *Approves* the decision of the Commission on the Status of Women to appoint a Special Rapporteur[1] to continue the study of the status of women and family planning and to report on the further measures that might be taken by the Commission in this field;

6. *Invites* the Special Rapporteur to take into account the information furnished in accordance with the present resolution.

17. POPULATION AND ITS RELATION TO ECONOMIC
    AND SOCIAL DEVELOPMENT: 1347 (XLV)[2]

The Economic and Social Council,

Noting the changes that have taken place in the world population situation in the last twenty years, caused by the considerable decline in mortality which has spurred world population growth,

Recognizing the importance of giving appropriate attention to the interrelations of economic, social and demographic factors in formulating development programmes,

Considering that the policy organs of relevant organizations in the United Nations system have stressed in their work programmes the importance of the problem,

Recognizing the need for the United Nations and the specialized agencies to assist the developing countries, upon request, in dealing with problems arising out of the current and prospective population trends, and in formulating and promoting national policies of their own choice in the field of population,

Considering that the International Conference on Human Rights held at Teheran adopted resolution XVIII of 12 May 1968 on human rights aspects of family planning, which states in part "that couples have a basic human right to decide freely and responsibly on the number and spacing of their children and a right to adequate education and information in this respect",

Taking into account the views of the Committee for Programme and Coordination, which recognizes the importance of demographic research and projects, and that such research should be restricted to studies which

---

[1] At its 1530th plenary meeting, the Council, in pursuance of paragraph 5 of the above resolution, appointed Mrs. Helvi L. Sipila (Finland) Special Rapporteur.

[2] Adopted unanimously 30 July 1968.

could serve as practical tools for policy-making or for supporting field activities and in particular that the United Nations population programme should concentrate more on information programmes at the regional and country levels.

. . .

Further noting the setting up of a United Nations Trust Fund for population activities as a measure to supplement the resources to be obtained from the regular budget and the United Nations Development Programme, and *welcoming* opportunities for strengthening these activities, made possible by additional voluntary resources,

. . .

3. *Recommends* that the United Nations Development Programme give due consideration to applications submitted for financing projects designed to assist developing countries in dealing with population problems, primarily in the fields of economic and social development, including both national and regional projects;

4. *Requests* the Secretary-General, within the approved programme of work, to:

(a) Pursue a programme of work covering training, research, information and advisory services in the field of fertility, mortality and morbidity, internal migration and urbanization and demographic aspects of economic and social development, in accordance with Council resolution 1084 (XXXIX) of 30 July 1965 and General Assembly resolution 2211 (XXI);

(b) Give special attention to further developing those aspects of the work in population fields which are of direct benefit to the developing countries, especially advice and technical assistance requested by Governments in population fields within the context of economic, social and health policies, and where appropriate, religious and cultural considerations;

(c) Submit to the General Assembly biennially a concise report on the world population situation, including an assessment of the current and prospective population trends;

(d) Bring promptly up to date the study *Determinants and Consequences of Population Trends;*

5. *Requests* the Committee on Development Planning to give appropriate attention to the interrelation between population dynamics and economic and social growth with respect to the second United Nations Development Decade, taking into account the diversity of regional and national characteristics;

6. *Invites* the regional economic commissions and the United Nations Economic and Social Office in Beirut to prepare and consider regional reports on population aspects of economic and social development;

7. *Welcomes* the decision of the Administrative Committee on Co-

ordination to establish a Sub-Committee on Population and *calls for* intensified action in cooperation with the Committee for Programme and Co-ordination to improve co-ordination and avoid duplication.

18. POPULATION POLICIES AND THE SECOND UNITED NATIONS DEVELOPMENT DECADE: 1483 (XLVIII)[1]

The Economic and Social Council,

. . .

Noting with appreciation the consideration of population policies for the Second United Nations Development Decade by the Committee for Development Planning,

Taking note of the deliberations of the Preparatory Committee for the Second United Nations Development Decade on a list of key areas in international cooperation for development during the Second Decade, including population, designed to fulfil the objectives for the Decade,

Recognizing the responsibility of the Population Commission to advise the Economic and Social Council on the interplay of demographic, economic and social factors and on any other population matters to which the organs of the United Nations or the specialized agencies may direct their attention,

1. *Calls upon* the Preparatory Committee for the Second United Nations Development Decade and the Committee for Development Planning to give full consideration to the deliberations and recommendations of the Population Commission at its fifteenth session, with special reference to the report on the world population situation, and to the population projections for 1965-1985;

2. *Calls upon* the Preparatory Committee for the Second United Nations Development Decade to give, as far as possible and if necessary, consideration to including in its development strategy the following text:

"In parts of the world, efforts during the Second United Nations Development Decade to promote long-term economic and social development adequate to improve the quality of life could be frustrated by the continuance of present high rates of population growth. In such cases, for countries which consider it appropriate and in accordance with the special needs of each country, national policies aimed at the achievement of more desirable rates of population growth and at the acceptance by parents on a voluntary basis of smaller families should be regarded as among the essential aspects of development strategy for the eventual achievement of satisfactory *per capita* economic growth, which would promote human welfare and dignity.";

---

[1]Adopted by 11 votes to 1, with 2 abstentions.

3. *Requests* the Secretary-General to continue to study, in consultation with relevant agencies, the relationship of population growth to economic and social development with special reference to the increase of gross national product and to improving national *per capita* income and standards of living, and to disseminate widely the major results of such studies.

19. THIRD WORLD POPULATION CONFERENCE: 1484 (XLVIII)[1]

The Economic and Social Council,

. . .

Considering that issues centering on population trends and structures are relevant to all countires, if in varying degrees — in some in so far as high rates of growth may be intensifying pressures of population on resources and in others in so far as rates of growth may fall short of those deemed to be consistent with economic and social development — and that the global review of population policies and exchange of knowledge and experience in actions will become more urgently needed with the advent of the 1970 census rounds and other sources which will become available from studies and operations carried out in the field of population,

. . .

1. *Approves* the proposal that a World Population Conference of representatives of Member States of the United Nations and members of specialized agencies be held under the auspices of the United Nations in 1974, and that participants consist of representatives of Member States of the United Nations and members of specialized agencies and their technical advisers as well as of other selected specialists;

2. *Decides* that the Conference shall be devoted to consideration of basic demographic problems, their relationship with economic and social development, and population policies and action programmes needed to promote human welfare and development;

3. *Requests* the Secretary-General in connexion with his plans for financing the World Population Converence:

(a) To seek provision in his 1971, 1972, 1973 and 1974 budget estimates for United Nations participation with the hope that adequate resources will be provided by the General Assembly;

(b) To explore the possibility of obtaining contributions from external sources so as to reduce the expenses incurred by the United Nations;

4. *Authorizes* the Secretary-General, in association with the executive heads of interested specialized agencies, and the non-governmental or-

---

[1]Adopted by 19 votes to 3, with 1 abstention, 3 April 1970.

ganizations involved in the study of population and of population problems to establish a small preparatory committee to assist in formulating an agenda based on the suggestions of the Population Commission as set forth in its report of the fifteenth session and making necessary arrangements for the Conference;

5. *Requests* the Conference to report to the Economic and Social Council and the General Assembly in 1975 on findings and recommendations of the deliberations at the Conference.

20. WORK PROGRAMMES AND PRIORITIES IN THE FIELD OF POPULATION: 1486 (XLVIII)[1]

The Economic and Social Council,
. . .

6. *Calls upon* all States Members of the United Nations and members of specialized agencies, in so far as it is practicable for them, to participate in the 1970 World Population Census Programme and to develop their vital statistics in accordance with the proposed World Programme for Improvement of Vital Statistics;

7. *Urges* interested Governments of States Members of the United Nations and members of specialized agencies to give full attention to population programmes in development planning and in policy-making and to utilize the available resources to this end;

8. *Requests* the Secretary-General in pursuing the work programme recommended by the Population Commission at its fifteenth session and in responding to requests from Governments:

(a) To observe such indications of priorities as have been given in the report of the Commission and in the Council;

(b) To pay special attention to technical cooperation at country and regional levels;

(c) To promote the 1970 round of population censuses and to assist, with all available resources, Governments, upon their request, in implementing them as an aid to development planning and policy-making;

(d) To undertake demographic studies needed for development planning and policy-making in developing countries;

(e) To conduct a second inquiry among the Governments of States Members of the United Nations and members of specialized agencies concerning population trends, economic and social development, and policies and action programmes taken by them;
. . .

---

[1]Adopted by 18 votes to 1, with 4 abstentions, 3 April 1970.

21. Principles and Recommendations for a Vital Statistics System: 1564 (L)[1]

The Economic and Social Council,

Noting that the Statistical Commission, at its sixteenth session, adopted a set of principles and recommendations for the improvement of vital statistics,

Recalling that paragraph 78 of the International Development Strategy for the Second United Nations Development Decade, adopted by the General Assembly in resolution 2626 (XXV) of 24 October 1970, provides that developing countries will, as appropriate, establish or strengthen their planning mechanisms, including statistical services, for formulating and implementing their national development plans during the Decade,

Also recalling General Assembly resolution 1710 (XVI) of 19 December 1961 on the United Nations Development Decade, in which the Assembly requested the Secretary-General to develop proposals for the intensification of action in the fields of economic and social development with particular reference to the need to review facilities for the collection, collation, analysis and dissemination of statistical and other information required for charting economic and social development and for providing a constant measurement of progress towards the objectives of the Decade,

Further recalling its resolution 1307 (XLIV) of 31 May 1968, in which the Council requested the Secretary-General to undertake a World Programme for the Improvement of Vital Statistics,

Recognizing the important role of vital statistics as a primary source of national data for achieving the above-mentioned purposes,

1. *Requests* the Secretary-General to publish the "Principles and recommendations for a vital statistics system" in English, French, Russian and Spanish and to distribute them widely to States Members of the United Nations or members of specialized agencies, to regional economic commissions and other appropriate regional bodies, and to specialized agencies;

2. *Further requests* the Secretary-General to give assistance to developing countries in the implementation of these principles and recommendations by mobilizing all available resources, both international and bilateral, to help in the very large task of assisting those countries to develop, improve and maintain civil registers of vital events and to use these registers for statistics as provided in the World Programme for the Improvement of Vital Statistics.

---

[1] Adopted unanimously 30 April 1971.

22. POPULATION AND DEVELOPMENT: 1672 (LII)[1]

The Economic and Social Council,

Recalling General Assembly resolution 2211 (XXI) of 17 December 1966 and the urgent need to take additional steps and measures for its full implementation,

Recalling also General Assembly resolution 2626 (XXV) of 24 October 1970, in which the Assembly recommended objectives, policies and measures needed to promote the economic and social progress of the developing nations, including, *inter alia,* demographic objectives and measures required for the Second United Nations Development Decade,

Aware that the Declaration on Social Progress and Development, proclaimed by the General Assembly in its resolution 2542 (XXIV) of 11 December 1969, confirmed that parents have the exclusive right to determine freely and responsibly the number and spacing of their children and that provision of knowledge and means necessary to enable them to exercise that right should be made available to individuals,

Noting that the General Assembly, in its resolution 2716 (XXV) of 15 December 1970, identified, as a minimum target for the Second United Nations Development Decade, availability of the necessary information and advice to all persons who so desire it to enable them to decide freely and responsibly on the number and spacing of their children and to prepare them for responsible parenthood,

Recalling General Assembly resolution 2683 (XXV) of 11 December 1970, by which the Assembly designated the year 1974 as World Population Year, as a way of focusing international attention on different aspects of the population problem and to provide an opportunity for Member States to make such efforts in the field of population as may be considered consistent with their respective needs,

Recalling also Economic and Social Council resolution 1484 (XLVIII) of 3 April 1970 on the third World Population Conference, 1974, in which the representatives of Member States would consider basic demographic problems, their relationship with economic and social development, and the population policies and action programmes needed,

Expressing its appreciation for the progress achieved in population activities by Member States and organizations of the United Nations system, and for the recent impressive increase in technical cooperation under the United Nations Fund for Population Activities,

Noting with appreciation the report entitled "Science and technology and problems of population growth in developing countries" submitted to the Economic and Social Council by the Advisory Committee on the Appliation of Science and Technology to Development,

---

[1]Adopted by 19 votes to none, with 7 abstentions, 2 June 1972.

Convinced that economic and social development is an essential element of and prerequisite to an effective population policy, and being aware that further action and expansion of activities is needed to this end at both the national and international levels,

Stressing that economic and social progress is the common and shared responsibility of each nation and the entire international community and that the obligations inherent in this responsibility are set down in the International Development Strategy for the Second United Nations Development Decade,

Being concerned with the immediate and long-range economic and social implications of rapid population growth as revealed in the projections of the United Nations,

A

1. *Urges* all Member States:

(a) To give full attention to their demographic objectives and measures during the biennial review and appraisal of the implementation of the Second United Nations Development Decade, and to take such steps as may be necessary to improve demographic statistics, research and planning machinery needed for development of population policies and programmes;

(b) To cooperate in achieving a substantial reduction of the rate of population growth in those countries which consider that their present rate of growth is too high and in exploring the possibility for the setting of targets for such a reduction in those countries;

(c) To ensure, in accordance with their national population policies and needs, that information and education about family palnning, as well as the means to practise family planning effectively, are made available to all individuals by the end of the Second United Nations Development Decade;

2. *Calls upon* all Member States, developed and developing alike, to give further support to the United Nations Fund for Population Activities in expanding the capacity of the United Nations system needed to promote activities in the population field in accordance with the objectives of the Second United Nations Development Decade;

3. *Calls upon* developed countries to provide, upon request, assistance in the population field without prejudice to other forms of development assistance;

4. *Calls upon* Member States and relevant United Nations bodies, in their present review and appraisal of the Second United Nations Development Decade, to give special attention to demographic, social and economic measures conducive to the achievement of the goals of the Decade;

5. *Requests* the Secretary-General:

(a) To initiate, in accordance with the spirit of the International Development Strategy for the Second United Nations Development Decade, studies needed for the development and implementation of demographic objectives and measures;

(b) To assist, upon request and in collaboration with the United Nations agencies concerned, Member States in population activities relevant to the biennial review and appraisal of the Second United Nations Decade.

B

1. *Endorses* in principle the draft programme and arrangements for the World Population Conference, 1974, as approved by the Population Commission at its sixteenth session;

2. *Decides* to assign to the Population Commission amongst its functions that of the intergovernmental preparatory body for the World Population Conference and the World Population Year and requests the Commission, in that capacity, to continue the preparatory work, taking into account actual and diverse situations prevailing in the various countries and regions, and to report back to the Council at its resumed fifty-third session in the first instance;

3. *Calls upon* States Members of the United Nations or members of specialized agencies or the International Atomic Energy Agency to take part in the World Population Conference and urges interested Member States to report on the actions they have taken in developing their population policies, programmes and activities;

4. *Decides* to place on the agenda of the World Population Conference a draft World Population Plan of Action and requests the Secretary-General to elaborate such a draft with the assistance of the Advisory Committee of Experts on Global Population Strategy decided upon at the sixteenth session of the population Commission;

5. *Requests* the Secretary-General, with the financial assistance of the United Nations Fund for Population Activities:

(a) To announce the World Population Year and World Population Conference at an early date and commend those programmes to the urgent attention of Governments of all Member States in order to emphasize that high priority should be given to the preparations for the Conference and the Year, and take such other steps as may be desirable for the attainment of the basic objectives of the Conference and the Year;

(b) To appoint, within the Department of Economic and Social Affairs and at the Assistant Secretary-General level, a Secretary-General for the World Population Conference and those World Population Year activities specifically related to the Conference, among them the symposia on population and development, human rights and the environment, equipped with the necessary secretariat resources, by drawing particularly upon the expertise and competence of the United Nations system as well as the Advisory Committee of Experts on Global Population Strategy;

(c) To designate the Executive Director of the United Nations Fund for Population Activities as having responsibility for preparations for the World Population Year and to request him to take the necessary steps, having regard to the resources available, to establish a secretariat from within the Fund and to work closely with the Population Division, the Centre for Economic and Social Information, the specialized agencies and the relevant non-governmental organizations;

6. *Urges* the Secretary-General of the Conference and the Executive Director of the Fund to cooperate to the extent necessary to ensure that preparations for the World Population Conference and the World Population Year proceed smoothly, bearing in mind the complementary nature of the activities of the Year and of the Conference.

C

1. *Approves* the proposed programme of measures and activities for the World Population Year, 1974, as recommended by the Population Commission at its sixteenth session;

2. *Invites* all Member States to take part in the observance of the World Population Year, especially to promote such activities as would improve knowledge and awareness as well as policies and measures relative to population and development;

3. *Calls the attention* of Governments of Member States to the valuable role which can be played by national population commissions in both developed and developing countries and which could enhance national population policies and programmes as well as national participation in the World Population Conference and World Population Year;

4. *Requests* the Secretary-General and the United Nations agencies concerned to render, upon request, all possible assistance to Member States to enable them to participate fully in accordance with their own policies in the activities of the World Population Year, including Technical assistance and aid by the United Nations Fund for Population Activities as requested by Member States;

5. *Requests* the Secretary-General to seek the widest possible cooperation of appropriate non-governmental organizations, research institutions and mass communication media in furthering the objectives of the World Population Year;

6. *Invites* the appropriate non-governmental organizations accredited to the Economic and Social Council, as well as national scientific and humanitarian organizations, to participate fully in the World Population Year.

D

1. *Endorses* the five-year and two-year programmes of work in the field of population recommended by the Population Commission at its sixteenth session, which include, *inter alia*, work to be done in connexion with the Second United Nations Development Decade, the World Population Conference, 1974, the World Population Year, 1974 and technical cooperation;

2. *Invites* the regional economic commissions and the United Nations Economic and Social Office at Beirut to develop further their five-year and two-year programmes of work in the population field in conformity with their particular regional needs, taking into account the recommendations of the Population Commission;

3. *Invites* the United Nations agencies concerned to develop further co-ordination and collaboration, in order to support population activities and the implementation of population programmes requested by Governments;

4. *Requests* the Secretary-General, in pursuing the programme of work recommended by the Population Commission at its sixteenth session and in response to requests from Member States:

(a) To give special attention to the development and improvement of demographic statistics;

(b) To draw particular attention to the need for taking measures as appropriate to speed up the implementation of the African Population Census Programme;

(c) To develop, in cooperation with the United Nations agencies concerned, appropriate measures needed to accelerate the review of requests for technical cooperation and implementation of technical assistance projects;

(d) To continue providing technical and financial support to the regional demographic training and research centres sponsored by the United Nations and to the development of the national population research capcaity;

(e) To assign priority to providing assistance for training of personnel, establishing national population research, advising on population policies and programmes and taking part in projects designed to support national population programmes;

(f) To make the necessary arrangements for the inclusion of population questions in the programmes of work of the United Nations Secretariat, with particular regard to population and social development, public administration, human rights and natural resources;

(g) To take such steps as may be necessary within the regular budget and extra-budgetary sources, to ensure that the programme of work, as recommended, could be fully implemented, particularly those projects directly related to the Second United Nations Development Decade, the World Population Conference, 1974, and the World Population Year, 1974;

5. *Requests* the Population Commission and the World Population Conference, 1974 to give the highest priority to the consideration of social, economic and other conditions conducive to the attainment of national demographic objectives.

23. STATUS OF THE UNMARRIED MOTHER: 1679 (LII)[1]

The Economic and Social Council,

Considering that the Charter of the United Nations, the Universal Declaration of Human Rights, the International Covenants on Human Rights, the Declaration on the Elimination of Discrimination against Women and the Declaration on Social Progress and Development have solemnly proclaimed and reaffirmed faith in fundamental human rights, in the dignity and worth of the human person and in the equal rights of men and women, and the determination to promote social progress and better standards of life,

Recalling that the principle of non-discrimination against women on account of maternity and of the protection of children is also embodied in these instruments and in the Declaration of the Rights of the Child,

Recalling also the adoption by the Economic and Social Council of resolution 1514 (XLVIII) of 28 May 1970 entitled "The unmarried mother and her child: their social protection and the question of their integration in society",

Noting that the ratio of unmarried mothers to married mothers is increasing in certain countries and that they are often subject to legal and social discrimination in violation of the principles of equality and non-discrimination set out in the above instruments,

Noting further the heavy responsibilities assumed by the unmarried mother,

Welcoming the recent emergence in most countries of a greater awareness of the difficulties confronting the unmarried mother,

Convinced that efforts should be made, through all possible means, to promote respect for the inherent dignity and worth of the human person, so as to enable all members of society, irrespective of marital status, to enjoy the equal and inalienable rights to which they are entitled, and contribute by their work to national development,

1. *Recommends* that Governments of Member States of the United Nations which have not yet done so, and which encounter this problem,

[1]Adopted by 23 votes to none, with 3 abstentions, 2 June 1972.

128

take all possible measures to eliminate any prevailing legal and social discrimination against the family consisting of an unmarried mother and her child and to offer such families all necessary advice and assistance, seeking to obtain a greater comprehension by society of their situation and with a view to eliminating the harm caused by lack of understanding and to securing them an acceptance on an equal footing with other members of society;

2. *Recommends* the following general principles for achieving that end:

(a) Maternal filiation shall be recognized in law, in all cases, automatically as a consequence of the fact of birth;

(b) Whatever the legal system applying in the case of married parents, the unmarried mother, whether paternal filiation is established or not, shall enjoy in all cases, as a parent, the fullest set of rights and duties provided for by law, in particular:

(i) If maternal filiation only is established, the surname of the mother should be transmitted to her child, if possible, in such a manner as not to reveal the fact of birth out of wedlock;

(ii) If maternal filiation only is established, the nationality of the unmarried mother shall be transmitted to her child as a consequence of the fact of birth; if both maternal and paternal filiations are established, the nationality of the child shall be governed by the same rules as those which apply in the case of birth in wedlock;

(iii) The unmarried mother should be vested in law with full parental authority over her child, in all cases, as an atuomatic consequence of the fact of birth; a family consisting of an unmarried mother and her child should not be subjected to any special control or supervision by the authorities different from that given to other families;

(iv) Maintenance rights and obligations as between the unmarried mother and her child should be the same as between a sole parent and a child born in wedlock; when both paternal and maternal filiations are established, the maintenance obligations of the parents to the child should be the same as if the child was born in wedlock; all appropriate assistance should be offered by the competent authority to the mother to help her (a) to establish paternal filiation and (b) to obtain an agreement by the father or a decision by the competent authority or court for the support of the child by his father; if the father does not fulfil his maintenance obligations, or if it is not possible to establish paternity, benefit should be available from appropriate public sources for the support of the mother and her child according to their needs;

(v) There should be no discrimination against the offspring of unmarried mothers in all matters of inheritance;

(vi) The unmarried mother should enjoy all the measures of social assistance and social security devised for mothers in general and for single parents in particular;

(vii) There should be no discrimination against the unmarried mother in matters of employment, education and training as well as in access to child care facilities;

3. *Recommends* that, where appropriate, consideration be given by Member States to the development of programmes designed to increase awareness of the existing double standard in allocating social responsibility for births out of wedlock, so as to bring about a balance in these social attitudes toward members of both sexes in the responsibility for such births.

B. Statistical Commission

1. Statistical Commission: 2/8

The Economic and Social Council, having considered the report of the Statistical Commission of 15 May 1946 (document E/39),
Decides that:

1. Functions

The functions of the Statistical Commission shall be those set forth in the terms of reference of the Commission as approved by the Economic and Social Council in its resolution of 16 February 1946 (document E/30), except for sub-paragraphs (a), (d), and (e) of paragraph 2, which are amended to read as follows:

(a) In promoting the development of national statistics and the improvement of their comparability;

(d) In advising the organs of the United Nations on general questions relating to the collection, interpretation and dissemination of statistical information;

(e) In promoting the improvement of statistics and statistical methods generally.

2. Composition

(a) The Statistical Commission shall consist of one representative from each of twelve Members[1] of the United Nations selected by the Council.

(b) With a view to securing a balanced representation in the various fields covered by the Commission, the Secretary-General shall consult

---

[1]The membership of the Statistical Commission was increased to 24 as from 4 August 1966.

with the Governments so selected before the representatives are finally nominated by these Governments and confirmed by the Council.

. . .

(f) The Economic and Social Council may in addition appoint, in their individual capacity, not more than twelve corresponding members from countries not represented on the Commission. Such members shall be appointed with the approval of the Governments concerned.

. . .

5. The Secretariat Statistical Unit

In organizing the Statistical Division in the Secretariat, the Secretary-General is requested to take into special consideration the recommendations of the Statistical Commission concerning:

(a) Organization of a central statistical unit in the Secretariat of the United Nations;

(b) Collection, analysis and evaluation of statistics from Member Governments, specialized agencies, and other sources;

(c) Publication of statistics;

(d) Co-ordination of statistical activities of specialized agencies;

(e) Promotion of development and improvement of statistics in general;

(f) Maintenance of an international centre for statistics;

(g) Maintenance of close contact and co-ordination with national Governments on programmes of statistical research, submission of statistical data, analysis and publication. The submission of statistical data, and their publication will be undertaken with the consent of the Governments concerned.

. . .

C. Population Commission

1. Population Commission: 3(III).

Resolution of 3 October 1946 supplemented by the action taken by the Council on 2 and 3 October 1946 concerning the appointment and tenure of office of the original members of the Commission (documents E/190/Rev.2, E/223, E/229).

The Economic and Social Council, requiring advice and assistance on matters affecting or affected by population changes in order to discharge the responsibilities vested in it by the Charter of the United Nations, establishes a Population Commission.[1]

---

[1]The membership of the Population Commission has been increased several times. At present the Commission consists of twenty-seven members elected by the Economic and Social Council for three-year terms.

1. The Population Commission shall arrange for studies and advise the Council on:

(a) Population changes, the factors associated with such changes, and the policies designed to influence these factors;

(b) Inter-relationships of economic and social conditions and population trends;

(c) Migratory movements of population and factors associated with such movements;

(d) Any other population problems on which the principal or subsidiary organs of the United Nations or the specialized agencies may seek advice.

. . .

6. The first task of the Population Commission shall be to draw up, with all reasonable speed, and submit to the Council for approval, a specific programme of work based in its terms of reference and taking into account any modifications in those terms of reference which the Commission may wish to recommend to the Council.

2. REPORT OF THE THIRD SESSION OF THE
POPULATION COMMISSION: 150 (VII)[1]

The Economic and Social Council,

Taking note of the report of the third session of the Population Commission, and

Having reconsidered the terms of reference for the Population Commission contained in Council resolution 3 (III),

Adopts the following in replacement thereof:

"The Population Commission shall arrange for studies and advise the Economic and Social Council on:

"(a) The size and structure of populations and the changes therein;

"(b) The interplay of demographic factors and economic and social factors;

"(c) Policies designed to influence the size and structure of populations and the changes therein;

"(d) Any other demographic questions on which either the principal or the subsidiary organs of the United Nations or the specialized agencies may seek advice."

D. SOCIAL COMMISSION

1. TEMPORARY SOCIAL COMMISSION: 2/10

Resolution adopted on 21 June 1946 (document E/78/Rev.1 and document E/84, paragraph 5, both as amended by the Council)

---

[1]Adopted 10 August 1948.

The Economic and Social Council, taking note of the recommendations of the Temporary Social Commission and bearing in mind the following considerations:

(a) The Economic and Social Council, in harmony with Article 55 of the Charter, shall endeavour to solve the international social problems, having in mind the connexion of these problems with the development of social activities in the national frame.

(b) The activities of the United Nations in the social field shall be based on democratic principles; these activities shall be conducted in the interest of all peoples concerned, and with the active participation of the organizations which unite groups of people concerned with such activities (trade unions of workers, agricultural societies, et cetera).

(c) The raising of the standard of living and the welfare of the peoples of the countries of the United Nations, which should include not only wages and income, but all kinds of social services, is an important task for the United Nations.

. . .

Establishes a permanent Social Commission.

1. Terms of Reference

The terms of reference of the Social Commission shall be:

(a) To advise the Council on social questions of a general character, and in particular on all matters in the social field not covered by specialized inter-governmental agencies;

(b) To advise the Council on practical measures that may be needed in the social field;

(c) To advise the Council on measures needed for the co-ordination of activities in the social field;

(d) To advise the Council on such international agreements and conventions on any of these matters, as may be required, and on their execution;

(e) To report to the Council on the extent to which the recommendations of the United Nations in the field of social policy are being carried out.

2. Composition

(a) The Social Commission shall consist of one representative from each of eighteen Members of the United Nations selected by the Council.

(b) With a view to securing a balanced representation in the various fields covered by the Commission, the Secretary-General shall consult with the Governments so selected before the representatives are finally nominated by these Governments and confirmed by the Council.

. . .

2. REAPPRAISAL OF THE ROLE OF THE SOCIAL COMMISSION: 1139(XLI)[1]

The Economic and Social Council,

. . .

Recalling General Assembly resolution 2035 (XX) of 7 December 1965, in which the Assembly requested the Council and the Social Commission, when considering the role which the United Nations should play in the social field, to bear in mind a number of general principles,

Convinced that the supreme goal of United Nations action in the social field is to assist in preparing a better future for man, in improving his well-being and in guaranteeing respect for his dignity,

Noting that, despite past efforts, the world social situation is far from satisfactory and therefore requires increased resources, improved methods and techniques of social action and a greater concentration of efforts on priority targets,

I

1. *Considers* that the social programme of the United Nations and the Social Commission should be undertaken with particular attention to the following considerations:

(a) The desirability of creating conditions of stability and well-being, necessary for peaceful and friendly relations among nations, based on respect for the principles of equal rights and self-determination of peoples; and of fulfilling the responsibilities of the Council set forth in Articles 55 and 58 of the Charter of the United Nations;

(b) The necessity of directing the main efforts of the United Nations in the social field towards supporting and strengthening independent social and economic development in the developing countries, with full respect for the permanent sovereignty of those countries over their natural resources, in accordance with General Assembly resolution 1803 (XVII) of 14 December 1962;

(c) The necessity of recognizing the inter-related character of economic and social factors and the basic requirement that economic development and social development should go together in the promotion of better standards of life in larger freedom, with full regard for both the importance of planning for achieving this end and for the role of Governments in promoting balanced and sound economic and social development;

(d) The necessity of mobilizing national resources and of encouraging creative initiatives of all peoples for achieving social progress;

(e) The significance of adequate structural social and economic changes for the achievement of social progress;

---

[1]Adopted 29 July 1966.

(f) The necessity of utilizing, to the widest possible extent, the experience of the developed and developing countries which have varying economic and social systems and which are at different stages of development;

2. *Reaffirms* that the Social Commission, bearing in mind the universal character of the United Nations, should give high priority and special attention to social development and to the needs of the developing countries;

3. *Reaffirms further* that close collaboration between the United Nations, the specialized agencies and the regional economic commissions is essential on the basis of the principles mentioned above;

4. *Considers* that, in future, the work programme of the Social Commission, as well as the programme of concerted practical action in the social field, should concentrate on all social aspects of programmes which further the following aims:

(a) The elimination of hunger and the raising of levels of health and nutrition;

(b) The improvement of standards of health and the extension of adequate health services to meet the needs of the whole population;

(c) The eradication of illiteracy, the extension and improvement of general and vocational education at all levels, and the improvement of access to educational and cultural facilities for all sectors of the population;

(d) The education of youth through the use of mass media and other educational methods in the spirit of peace, in order to combat those influences which lead to undesirable social trends and to juvenile delinquency;

(e) The raising of levels of employment and income in both rural and urban areas, with particular attention, where appropriate, to employment opportunities for young people;

(f) The improvement of housing conditions and of community services, especially for persons in low-income groups, urban development and planning for future urban growth;

(g) The provision of social welfare and of comprehensive social security services to maintain and improve the standard of living of families, individuals and special groups, including the disabled, with special attention to working mothers and to the establishment of adequate provision for children, as well as to the strengthening and improvement of the quality of family life;

(h) The study of social aspects of industrialization, with a view to encouraging the rapid expansion of industrialization, together with the study of urbanization, with attention also to family disruption;

(i) The allocation of an increased proportion of the national budgetary provision for social and cultural purposes;

5. *Considers* that, in pursuit of these objectives, particular attention should be paid by the United Nations, the Governments of Member States and the specialized agencies to the use of effective methods and techniques such as:

(a) Planning of social development in conjunction with economic development, with a view to attaining balanced and integrated economic and social development;

(b) Training of national cadres for development, including administrative, professional and technical personnel, and specialists in the social field;

(c) Recognizing the role of the State and the public sector in promoting balanced and sound economic and social development and in raising the welfare of the population;

(d) Establishing where appropriate in co-operation with the Population Commission, action programmes in the field of population consistent with the economic, social, religious and cultural circumstances of the respective countries;

(e) Mobilizing human resources through co-operatives and governmental and non-governmental organizations as well as through community development and planned regional development;

(f) Promoting social reforms basic to the achievement of high levels of living and economic and social progress, in particular agrarian reforms, equitable distribution of the national income and social advancement of certain racial or ethnic groups or individuals requiring social protection;

6. *Recommends* that the Social Commission, to further these objectives, give special attention to:

(a) The periodic reports on the world social situation;

(b) Studies of the social consequences of disarmament;

(c) Studies of the influence on social development of fair international trade;

II

Believes, in view of the aforementioned considerations:

(a) That the United Nations and the specialized agencies, while seeking means of increasing technical co-operation services in order to meet the ever-growing needs of the developing countries, should concentrate their technical assistance in the social field on the priority sectors of the requesting countries, the order of priority being established by Governments in accordance with their general economic and social development planning;

(b) That a larger share of the available resources of the United Nations and the specialized agencies should be devoted to operational activites, in order to meet the urgent needs of the developing countries;

(c) That studies and research done by the United Nations and the specialized agencies should result in practical action;

(d) That the Social Commission, in order to give the Economic and Social Council pertinent advice on social policies designed to establish social targets and priorities, should regularly receive reports prepared by the specialized agencies and the technical co-operation services of the United Nations on the results obtained and the difficulties encountered in the course of such assistance;

. . .

IV

1. *Decides* that the Social Commission shall retain its status as a functional commission of the Economic and Social Council but shall be redesignated the Commission for Social Development, to clarify its role as a preparatory body of the Council in the whole range of social development policy; the Member States elected to the Commission should nominate, to serve on the Commission for a period of three years, candidates who hold key positions in the planning or execution of national social development policies or other persons qualified to discuss the formulation of social policies in more than one sector of development;

2. *Decides also* that the Commission for Social Development may establish such sub-committees as may be authorized by the Council in conformity with Article 66 of the rules of procedure of the functional commissions of the Council;

3. *Further decides* that the Commission for Social Development shall advise the Council also on vital social problems in respect of which action or recommendations may be required either by the Council itself or by the General Assembly in accordance with General Assembly resolution 2035 (XX);

. . .

E.   COMMISSION ON HUMAN RIGHTS

1.   COMMISSION ON HUMAN RIGHTS AND SUB-COMMISSION
ON THE STATUS OF WOMEN: 1/5

Resolution of the Economic and Social Council of 16 February 1946 (document E/20 of 15 February 1946), on the establishment of a Commission on Human Rights and a Sub-Commission on the Status of Women, supplemented by the action taken by the Council on 18 February 1946, completing paragraphs 6 and 7 of section A and paragraphs 4 and 5 of section B concerning the initial composition of these bodies.

Section A.

1. *The Economic and Social Council,* being charged under the Charter with the responsibility of promoting universal respect for, and observance of, human rights and fundamental freedoms for all without distinction as to race, sex, language or religion, and requiring advice and assistance to enable it to discharge this responsibility,

Establishes a Commission on Human Rights.

2. The work of the Commission shall be directed towards submitting proposals, recommendations and reports to the Council regarding:

(a) An international bill of rights;

(b) International declarations or conventions on civil liberties, the status of women, freedom of information and similar matters;

(c) The protection of minorities;

(d) The prevention of discrimination on grounds of race, sex, language or religion.

3. The Commission shall make studies and recommendations and provide information and other services at the request of the Economic and Social Council.

. . .

6. Initially, the Commission shall consist of a nucleus of nine members appointed in their individual capacity for a term of office expiring on 31 March 1947. They are eligible for re-appointment. . . .

. . .

2. COMMISSION ON HUMAN RIGHTS: 2/9[1]

Resolution adopted on 21 June 1946 (documents E/56/Rev.1 and E/84, paragraph 4, both as amended by the Council).

The Economic and Social Council, having considered the report of the nuclear Commission on Human Rights of 21 May 1946 (document E/38/Rev.1)

Decides as follows:

1. FUNCTIONS

The functions of the Commission on Human Rights[2] shall be those set forth in the terms of reference of the Commission, approved by the Economic and Social Council in its resolution of 16 February 1946, with the addition to paragraph 2 of that resolution of a new sub-paragraph (e) as follows:

(e) Any other matter concerning human rights not covered by items (a), (b), (c) and (d).

. . .

---

[1]Adopted unanimously, 21 June 1946.

[2]The membership of the Commission on Human Rights was increased to 32 for three-year terms as of 4 August 1966.

4. Documentation

The Secretary-General is requested to make arrangements for:

(a) The compilation and publication of a year-book on law and usage relating to human rights, the first edition of which should include all declarations and bills on human rights now in force in the various countries;

(b) The collection and publication of i formation on the activities concerning human rights of all organs of the United Nations;

. . .

(d) The preparation and publication of a survey of the development of human rights;

(e) The collection and publication of plans and declarations on human rights by specialized agencies and non-governmental national and international organizations.

. . .

F. Commission on the Status of Women

1. Commission on the Status of Women: 2/11[1]

The Economic and Social Council, having considered the report of the nuclear Commission on Human Rights and of the nuclear Sub-Commission on the Status of Women of 21 May 1946 (document E/38/Rev. 1),

Decides to confer upon the Sub-Commission the status of a full commission to be known as the Commission on the Status of Women.

1. Functions

The functions of the Commission shall be to prepare recommendations and reports to the Economic and Social Council on promoting women's rights in political, economic, social and educational fields. The Commission shall also make recommendations to the Council on urgent problems requiring immediate attention in the field of women's rights.

The Commission may submit proposals to the Council regarding its terms of reference.

2. Composition

(a) The Commission on the Status of Women shall consist of one representative from each of fifteen Members of the United Nations selected by the Council.[2]

(b) With a view to securing a balanced representation in the various fields covered by the Commission, the Secretary-General shall consult

---

[1]Adopted unanimously 21 June 1946.

[2]The membership of the Commission on the Status of Women has been increased several times. The Commission presently consists of thirty-two members elected by the Economic and Social Council for four-year terms.

with the Governments so selected before the representatives are finally
nominated by these Governments and confirmed by the Council.
. . .

2. Family Planning: Resolution 4 (XIX) of the Commission on the Status of Women[1]

The Commission on the Status of Women.
. . .

Believing that expanded research with regard to family planning will
be of great value, and that educational information which can be expected to result from this research should be available to women in developed
as well as in developing countries,

1. *Invites* the Secretary-General to include in the report he is preparing for the twentieth session of this Commission on the relation between family planning and the advancement of women, a brief summary
of pertinent research and resources available through the United Nations, with special emphasis on informational material which might be
used in conferences of non-governmental as well as of official bodies;

2. *Welcomes* the increasing recognition of the role of United Nations
agencies in providing assistance, upon the request of Governments, in
educational programmes concerned with the planning of families.

G. Advisory Committee on the Application of Science and Technology to Development (ACAST)

1. Questions Relating to Science and Technology: 980 (XXXVI)[2]

A

Report of the Secretary-General on the Results of the
United Nations Conference on the Application of Science
and Technology for the Benefit of the Less Developed Areas

The Economic and Social Council,
. . .

4. *Decides* to establish an advisory committee on the application of
science and technology to development, consisting of fifteen members

---

[1]Adopted by 11 votes to none, with 8 abstentions, 4 March 1966.
[2]Adopted 1 August 1963.

appointed by the Council, on the nomination of the Secretary-General after consultation with Governments, on the basis of their personal qualifications, knowledge or experience in this field, with due regard to equitable geographical representation, the committee to have the following functions:

(a) To keep under review progress in the application of science and technology and propose to the Council practical measures for such application for the benefit of the less developed areas;

(b) To review, in close cooperation with the Administrative Committee on Co-ordination, the scientific and technological programmes and activities of the United Nations and related agencies and propose to the Council measures for their improvement, including the establishment of priorities and the elimination of duplication;

(c) To consider specific questions referred to it by the Council, or by the Secretary-General, or by the executive heads of the specialized agencies and the International Atomic Energy Agency;

(d) To study and to advise the Council as to the need for making changes of organization or other arrangements which would advance the application of science and technology for the benefit of developing countires;[1]

. . .

---

[1] The Economic and Social Council by its Resolution 1621 (LI), "Organization of the Work of the Council: B. Institutional Arrangements for Science and Technology," increased the membership of the Advisory Committee to twenty-four, and decided that the Advisory Committee should furnish its expertise to the Council's newly-established Standing Committee for matters relating to science and technology.

PART FIVE

REGIONAL ECONOMIC COMMISSIONS

A.   Economic Commission for Europe (ECE)

1.   Terms of Reference and Rules of Procedure: E/ECE/778/Rev.1

1. The Economic Commission for Europe, acting within the framework of the policies of the United Nations and subject to the general supervision of the Council, shall, provided that the Commission takes no action in respect to any country without the agreement of the Government of that country:

(a) Initiate and participate in measures for facilitating concerted action for the economic reconstruction of Europe, for raising the level of European economic activity, and for maintaining and strengthening the economic relations of the European countries both among themselves and with other countries of the world;

(b) Make or sponsor such investigations and studies of economic and technological problems of and developments within member countries of the Commission and within Europe generally as the Commission deems appropriate;

(c) Undertake or sponsor the collection, evaluation and dissemination of such economic, technological and statistical information as the Commission deems appropriate.

. . .

4. The Commission is empowered to make recommendations on any matter within its competence directly to its member Governments, Governments admitted in a consultative capacity . . . , and the specialized agencies concerned. The Commission shall submit for the Council's prior consideration any of its proposals for activities that would have important effects on the economy of the world as a whole.

. . .

B.   Economic Commission for Asia and the Far East (ECAFE)

1.   Terms of Reference[1]

---

[1]As adopted by the Economic and Social Council at its fourth session and amended by the Council at subsequent sessions, including the fifty-first and fifty-second and revised in consequence of various General Assembly resolutions on the admission of new Members.

The Economic and Social Council,

Having considered General Assembly resolution 46 (I) of 11 December 1946, in which the General Assembly "recommends that, in order to give effective aid to the countries devastated by war, the Economic and Social Council, at its next session, give prompt and favourable consideration to the establishment of . . . an Economic Commission for Asia and the Far East," and

Having noted the report of the Working Group for Asia and the Far East of the Temporary Sub-Commission on Economic Reconstruction of Devastated Areas,

Establishes an Economic Commission for Asia and the Far East with terms of reference as follows:

1. The Economic Commission for Asia and the Far East, acting within the framework of the policies of the United Nations and subject to the general supervision of the Council, shall, provided that the Commission takes no action in respect of any country without the agreement of the Government of that country;

(a) Initiate and participate in measures for facilitating concerted action for the economic reconstruction and development of Asia and the Far East, for raising the level of economic activity in Asia and the Far East and for maintaining and strengthening the economic relations of these areas both among themselves and with other countries of the world;

(b) Make or sponsor such investigations and studies of economic and technological problems and developments within territories of Asia and the Far East as the Commission deems appropriate;

(c) Undertake or sponsor the collection, evaluation and dissemination of such economic, technological and statistical information as the Commission deems appropriate;

(d) Perform such advisory services, within the available resources of its secretariat, as the countries of the region may desire, provided that such services do not overlap with those rendered by the specialized agencies or the United Nations Technical Assistance Administration;

(e) Assist the Economic and Social Council, at its request, in discharging its functions within the region in connexion with any economic problems including problems in the field of technical assistance;

(f) In carrying out the above functions, deal, as appropriate, with the social aspects of economic development and the interrelationship of the economic and social factors.

. . .

8. The Commission is empowered to make recommendations on any matters within its competence directly to the Governments of members or associate members concerned, Governments admitted in consultative capacity, and the specialized agencies concerned. The Commission shall

submit for the Council's prior consideration any of its proposals of activities that would have important effects on the economy of the world as a whole.

. . .

2. RESOLUTION AND RECOMMENDATIONS OF THE ASIAN POPULATION CONFERENCE PERTINENT TO POLICIES AND PROGRAMMES OF GOVERNMENTS AND INTERNATIONAL ORGANIZATIONS[1]

The Asian Population Conference,

Recognizing that the problems of population and social and economic development are interrelated and that the acceleration of social and economic progress is in its turn of great importance to the removal of obstacles created by high rates of population growth,

I. NATIONAL POLICY AND ACTION

Considering

(a) That the rapid growth of population in many countries of the ECAFE region is impeding their economic and social development and threatening the success of their efforts to reach satisfactory levels of living within a tolerable length of time,

(b) that the high proportion of young children in the population which results from a high birth rate is an impediment to progress especially in the education field,

(c) that rapid growth of population in the countryside increases pressure on the land, while any consequent acceleration in migration creates additional problems of social and economic adjustment,

Invites the Governments of States Members of the Economic Commission for Asia and the Far East:

(a) to take account of the urgency of adopting a positive population policy related to their individual needs and to the general needs of the region;

(b) to take account of the recommendations of this Conference relating to national population policies in the formulation and execution of their general policies and plans for social and economic development;

II. INTERNATIONAL COOPERATION

Further noting that the efforts to find satisfactory and effective solutions to population problems are hampered in many countries in the region by lack of facilities and funds, of technical assistance, and of com-

---

[1]Adopted unanimously 20 December 1963.

prehensive and reliable demographic statistics, and by insufficient development of demographic and socio-biological research and shortage of personnel with appropriate training and experience,

Recalling the recommendations of the General Assembly in its resolution 1838 (XVII) of 18 December 1962 favouring intensified research on interrelationships of population growth and social and economic development, with particular reference to the developing countries, and of the Economic and Social Council in its resolution of April 1963 inviting regional and economic commissions to examine possibilities of intensifying their work in the demographic field,

Requests the Executive Secretary to take note of the recommendations of this Conference, with a view to:

(a) facilitating direct exchange of information at the departmental level among Governments within the region on all aspects of population and social and economic growth,

(b) expanding the scope of technical assistance available to Governments in the region, upon their request, for data collection, research, experimentation and action on all aspects of population problems, including family welfare planning programmes, through regional advisory services, development and strengthening of regional, sub-regional and national training and research institutions, study tours, fellowships and meetings of technical groups,

(c) expanding the services of the ECAFE secretariat in the field of population,

Strongly requests the Economic Commission for Asia and the Far East to give its full support to the recommendations of this Conference.

Recommendations

The following recommendations were unanimously adopted:

A. *National population policies*

The Conference agreed on the importance of demographic factors in the problems of economic and social development, especially of the less-developed countries in the ECAFE region. Rapid population growth in many of these countries is impeding the progress of economic and social development and threatening the success of efforts to reach satisfactory levels of living within a tolerable length of time. The high proportion of dependent children in the population which results from the high birth rate in the majority of ECAFE countries is also an impediment to progress, especially in fulfilling education targets. The rapid growth of population in the countryside increases pressure on the land, while any consequent acceleration of migration creates additional problems of social and economic adjustment. The problems of population and social and economic development are interrelated and acceleration of social and economic progress is, in turn, of great importance to the removal of obstacles created by high rates of population growth.

Each country in the region has its own population problems. No single prescription for population policy would be suitable in view of the differences among countries in size, density and rate of growth of the population, national resources and other conditions of the economy, and characteristics of national culture. As the General Assembly of the United Nations has declared, it is for each Government to decide its own policy in this sphere. At the same time, the policy adopted and the actions taken by each Government to deal with the national problems of population and economic and social development are of common concern to all nations, as all have a stake in the success of efforts to achieve satisfactory conditions of life for all the world's peoples with a minimum of delay.

The Asian Population Conference therefore recommends to the Governments in the region and to ECAFE the following general principles with regard to the formulation and implementation of national population policies;

(a) Each Government should decide what kinds of action, if any, should be taken to moderate the rate of population growth and to influence the distribution of population within the country as an aid to satisfactory progress in economic and social development.

(b) Such decisions should be based on an appraisal of the country's demographic situation and prospects and of the interrelationships between population trends and economic and social development. Periodic appraisals, including short- and long-term population projections, taking into account the trends of population and changing economic and social circumstances, the establishment of the necessary foundation of demographic and other statistics and the development of pertinent research, should have high priority.

(c) Measures aimed at influencing the growth or distribution of population should not be considered as substitutes for efforts to develop resources, improve technology and expand production, but as complementary means of raising the levels of living of the people.

(d) A national population policy should be integrated with policies and programmes in related economic and social spheres, such as education, health, nutrition, social welfare, social security, housing, status of women, agricultural and industrial development and manpower utilization. The effects of contemplated development in these various spheres upon population trends, as well as the effects of population changes upon economic and social development, should be taken into account in formulating development plans.

(e) Because the trend of demographic factors generally changes slowly and the cumulative effect of its changes over a long period of time may be very great, population policies should be formulated in the long-range perspective of future developments in the national economy and social conditions and of future manpower and consumer goods requirements.

B. International cooperation

Shortage of personnel with training and experience in demography and related fields handicaps the development of needed demographic data, research, experimental work and programmes of action relating to population problems in many countries of the region. Facilities for training such personnel are also insufficiently developed in much of the region, although a few ECAFE countries have institutions for specialized training in demography and allied fields. Technical assistance and other forms of regional and inter-regional cooperation can do much towards overcoming these handicaps. The demographic work of ECAFE and the United Nations and the related activities of other international organizations must be expanded if the need of the less-developed countries for assistance in dealing with their population problems is to be met.

The Asian Population Conference therefore makes the recommendations outlined below for international cooperation in this field:

(1) The United Nations and its specialized agencies should expand the scope of the technical assistance which they are prepared to give at the request of Governments in the development of statistics, research, experimentation and action programmes relating to population problems.

(2) Multilateral consultations should be held among those Governments in the ECAFE region and elsewhere which are interested in obtaining assistance in family planning activities and those which are interested in providing such assistance.

(3) ECAFE's regional advisory services in the demographic field should be strengthened as early as possible in view of the limitations of technical assistance resources. A team of advisers with varied types of experience relevant to population problems should be made available upon request to assist the staff of government agencies and research institutions in countries of the region. This team should include experts in demographic, sociological and economic research, surveys and experimental work on problems of motivation and communication.

(4) Regional facilities for demographic training and research should be strengthened so as to serve the needs of countries in the region as fully as possible. . . .

. . .

(9) ECAFE should strengthen the staff in its secretariat assigned to work on population matters so as to be in a position to render effective services to the government agencies and institutions working in this field throughout the region. Among the activities recommended for the ECAFE secretariat are:

(a) Assembling and analysing statistical data and other information on the demography of countries in the region, and preparing reports for publication on various aspects of the demographic situation and prospects in the region as a whole and the interrelation of population trends with social and economic development.

(b) Maintaining a list of demographic research and training institutions in countries within the region and of their activities, and promoting cooperation and division of labour among them, with a view to enhancing comparability of research findings and improving the efficiency of research and training activities in the region as a whole.

(c) Arranging for fundamental research on population questions to be carried out by universities and research institutions within the region and for publication of the results of such research.

C. Questions of economic and social policy and planning relevant to population problems

1. Agricultural development and food supply

The increase in food production in the ECAFE countries since the Second World War together with significant increases in imports of food has been barely sufficient to restore pre-war per capita levels of food consumption. In view of the large increase of population foreseen for the next two decades and the urgent need to raise national nutritional levels, it is imperative to step up the rate of growth of agricultural production, with due attention to the various components of food intake. . . .

. . .

2. Health programmes

Although death rates have been reduced drastically during the last few years in most of the ECAFE region, the public health facilities available in many countries are still only elementary. With the high levels of infant mortality, high proportions of deaths from communicable diseases, high death rates from intestinal diseases attributable mainly to the lack of environmental sanitation and safe water supply, and high death rates of females in the reproductive ages, the need for further development of health programmes is apparent. This work, as well as economic and social efforts to improve the levels of living of the population, is adversely affected by the rapid growth of population.

Nevertheless, substantial and rapid reductions in mortality have been achieved by improving medical and health services in many parts of the region, and where, as in most ECAFE countries, there is an absence of corresponding reductions in fertility, the result has been increasing rates of population growth. A similar trend is also imminent in the remaining areas of the region where mortality is still relatively high. It is recognized that improvement in health, as in other components of levels of living, may be jeopardized or at least retarded by too rapid population growth.

The Conference therefore recommends:

(a) Research on the changing health needs occasioned by current and prospective demographic trends, and on the demographic consequences of health programmes, should be intensified at the national level.

(b) In addition to national efforts, international agencies should direct more attention to the study and evaluation of demographic aspects of health problems in the ECAFE region.

(c) As an aid to expansion of study and research in this field, national data on mortality and morbidity must be improved; at least until adequate facilities render this unnecessary, consideration should be given to the use of temporary measures such as nomenclatures and classification of diseases for non-medical personnel.

(d) In countries where it is found desirable and feasible to encourage measures for the moderation of fertility as a means of promoting family welfare and health, such measures should be provided for when planning or extending health services.

The Conference recognizes that health needs are served not only by medical, but also by other social and economic programmes and activities, and that the consequences to health of social and economic changes are very considerable. It therefore considers important the integration of health programmes with over-all development plans for each nation, and emphasizes the need for long-term programming of personnel training and provision of utilities, facilities and services, taking into account the changing needs in the future, so that the long-term as well as short-term returns from investments in health may be maximized.

3. Social welfare problems

Several aspects of population trends are of direct consequence in planning social welfare services. Of great importance in this regard is the age structure of population and its distribution between rural and urban communities.

Persistent high levels of fertility in most of the ECAFE countries have produced a "young" population, and the migration to the cities is producing an increasing degree of urbanization throughout the region. Therefore, Governments in the region should include in their development programmes provision for social welfare services specifically directed towards:

(1) Expansion of child welfare services in view of the increasing numbers of children;

(2) Formulation of certain types of family welfare services such as family allowances, marriage guidance, etc.;

(3) Measures to regulate child labour and to ease problems relating to participation of women in suitable occupations; and

(4) Planning of urban development projects, including adequate housing for immigrants and needy groups.

4. *Education programmes*

Attainment of the social and economic objectives of the countries of the region will require fuller utilization of human as well as physical resources. Education planning, therefore, should be an integral part of social and economic development planning. The present rapid growth of the school-age population in most ECAFE countries, which will continue as long as the decline in mortality is not matched by a decline in fertility, profoundly affects the problem of raising the educational level of coming generations. Such rapid growth also adds to the difficulties of qualitatively up-grading education, as it creates a heavy demand for primary schools and teachers. Removal of the bottleneck in secondary level education is also made more difficult by the rapid growth in the primary school-age population.

The Conference recognizes that there is a two-way relationship between population growth and education development and urges Governments in the region to consider, when formulating their development policies, not only the effect of population growth upon educational needs and problems, but also the possible effects of increasing education upon fertility, migration and population growth and distribution. The Conference recommends that ECAFE in conjunction with the specialized agencies, expand its activities to include:

(a) investigation of the role of demographic studies in education planning and of the requirements of demographic data and methodological problems in this connexion;

(b) studies of the effects of education upon population trends through such intermediaries as:

(i) effects upon child labour;

(ii) effects on the real costs of child-rearing to the family and upon motivation for family limitation;

(iii) effects on age of marriage;

(iv) effects on problems of communicating new ideas relating to family welfare and family planning, etc.;

(v) effects on health and mortality;

(vi) effects on the volume and characteristics of internal migration.

5. *Problems of economic growth*

By the early 1960's real *per capita* national product in most of the ECAFE countries had recovered to levels at best slightly higher than prior to the second World War, and in some cases somewhat lower. While such limited progress is perhaps understandable in view of the serious handicaps of low initial levels of health and education, wartime disruption and problems associated with the transition to political independence, it is disappointing to the aspirations of the nations concerned. It was recognized, however, that growth potential, as distinct from accomplishment, in these countries had increased as a result of improvements in human and material resources and in the institutional environment.

Policies with regard to demographic aspects of economic growth involve the role of both population numbers and population quality in economic development. At the heart of the process of economic development is the growth and diffusion of knowledge and its application to methods of production. A poorly educated population, enervated by malnutrition and disease and inadequately sheltered, has neither the vigour nor capabilities necessary to master new techniques. On the other hand, a healthy, educated population under appropriate institutional conditions is alert to possibilities of adopting new methods and is capable, when necessary, of working out new solutions appropriate to its particular conditions. Thus the policies outlined in preceding sections, particularly to improve the human resources of the ECAFE countries, are critical for achievement of the goal of economic growth. For this as well as other reasons, the Conference urges Governments in the region to accord high priority to such policies.

There is a great need for research to clarify more fully the specific interrelations between human resources and the process of economic growth. For this purpose, further development of basic data is required, including not only the standard types of demographic and manpower data, but also data bearing on social conditions of the population and on scientific and intellectual resources, such as the data employed in the work of the United Nations Bureau of Social Affairs and UNESCO. Such research involves also the initiation of studies of actual conditions surrounding the diffusion of new methods of production, of mortality and fertility control, and new institutional devices. Such conditions embrace the characteristics of the population, the channels of communication of new knowledge, and institutional conditions. This research of necessity calls for attention to sub-national demographic units and should benefit from attention to the historical experience both of developed and developing countries.

6. Policies designed to promote fuller utilization of human resources

The Conference paid special attention to the problems of inadequate utilization of human resources of many countries in the region, including problems of underemployment and unemployment as well as shortage of skilled manpower. These problems would remain even if success were achieved in reducing fertility within a short period as there would be an inevitable time lag in the effect of falling birth rates on the growth of labour supply. . . .

. . .

154

7. Programmes relating to fertility and family planning

In view of the rapid rates of population growth, several Governments in the region, including those of India, Pakistan and the Republic of Korea, have made family planning a national policy. Other Governments in the region are assisting voluntary organizations in family planning work. Still others have expressed concern about the consequences of high birth rates for mothers' health and family welfare as well as national social and economic development.

The Asian countries which have made family planning a part of national policy are handicapped in their efforts to put it into effect by lack of experience and pertinent knowledge. Each Government is developing its programme to suit national needs in keeping with the cultural values of different sections of the population. To accelerate progress towards the goals of family planning programmes, the Conference recommends that Governments which have undertaken such programmes or are contemplating them should pool their knowledge and experience of communication of ideas on family planning and adoption of family planning methods.

The Conference considered some of the statistical aspects of evaluation of family planning programmes and emphasized the need for improvement of vital statistics in many countries in the region. The need for development of sensitive indices for measuring small changes in fertility resulting from organized programmes was also brought out. The discussions at the Conference disclosed that there were no cultural or religious objections to responsible parenthood and regulation of family size in most of the ECAFE countries. Methods of regulation are available which would be compatible with every value system.

In programmes aimed at promoting family planning, individuals should in all cases be left free to select the methods which they prefer for spacing and limiting births, in accordance with their religious convictions and other preferences.

While action programmes could be immediately started on the basis of available knowledge, note was taken of the limitations of both social science and biological and medical knowledge relevant to promotion of family planning. In the social sciences, it is necessary to learn more about the sociological and social-psychological aspects of family planning. In the bio-medical sciences, there is need for more knowledge of the physiology of human reproduction so as to devise more acceptable, practical and effective methods of regulating the number and spacing of births.

8. Policies and programmes relating to urbanization, internal migration and population distribution

The Conference recommends that Governments in the ECAFE region take into consideration, in planning for urban and rural development:

(a) The existing and the prospective future balance in population distribution as between urban and rural sectors, as well as regional areas;

(b) The impact of development programmes in the urban and rural sectors on internal migration and on the rate of urbanization; and

(c) The consequences of urbanization and its role in the development of national economy.

. . .

3. POPULATION GROWTH AND ECONOMIC AND SOCIAL DEVELOPMENT: 54 (XX)[1]

The Committee of the Whole of the Economic Commission for Asia and the Far East,

Considering that the achievement of a satisfactory pattern of economic growth, including advancement in health, nutrition, housing, education, social welfare and the whole range of social services, is a vital necessity for the region,

Considering further that any economic and social development programme should take into account and, if necessary, modify demographic trends in view of their interrelationship with economic and social processes,

Recognizing that the recent demographic trends amongst most of the countries of the region, which reflect high rates of population growth and an increasing mobility of the population, are hindering the achievement of satisfactory living standards in the shortest possible time,

Noting further that the problems relating to the increase in the volume of migration within countries, especially from rural to urban areas, require even greater efforts on the part of Governments to achieve urgently needed economic and social betterment,

Observing that efforts to find effective solutions for population problems have been hampered in many countries of the region by lack of facilities and funds, lack of comprehensive and reliable demographic statistics, insufficient development of demographic and socio-biological research and shortages of trained personnel, all of which have heightened the need for international or intra-regional cooperation.

Recalling General Assembly resolution 1838 (XVII) of 18 December 1962, recommending that the Economic Commission for Asia and the Far East intensify study and research on the interrelationship of population growth and economic and social development, and endorsing the view of the Population Commission that the United Nations should encourage and assist developing countries in obtaining basic data and carrying out studies of the demographic aspects of development,

---

[1]Adopted unanimously 17 March 1964.

Recalling Economic and Social Council resolution 933 (XXXV) of 5 April 1963, inviting the Economic Commission for Asia and the Far East to examine the possibilities of intensifying its work in the demographic field within the general framework of the programme recommended by the Population Commission at its twelfth session,

Noting with approval the resolution unanimously adopted by the Asian Population Conference on 20 December 1963, strongly urging the Economic Commission for Asia and the Far East to give its full support to the recommendations of the Conference,

1. *Invites* the Governments of Member States of the Economic Commission for Asia and the Far East:

(a) To take account of the urgent need to adopt a positive population policy related to their individual needs,

(b) To take account, in their formulation and execution of general policies and plans for social and economic development, of the recommendations of the Asian Population Conference relating to national population policies;

2. *Requests* the Executive Secretary to:

(a) Facilitate direct exchanges of information at the departmental level among Governments in the region on all aspects of population and social and economic growth,

(b) Expand the scope of technical assistance available to Governments in the region, upon their request, for data collection, research, experimentation and action in all aspects of population problems, including family welfare planning programmes, through regional advisory services, development and strengthening of regional, sub-regional and national training and research institutions, study tours, fellowships and meetings of technical groups;

3. *Further requests* the Executive Secretary to organize a collaborative programme of regional, sub-regional and inter-regional technical working group meetings designed to provide guidelines for governmental action and international assistance in particular fields of work relating to the population problems of the region;

4. *Recommends* that the Conference of Asian Statisticians give urgent attention to inadequacies in the concepts and definitions of the labour force, employment, unemployment and under-employment as used in the statistics of countries of the region;

5. *Invites* the United Nations and the specialized agencies to expand the scope of the technical assistance they are prepared to give, upon the request of Governments, in the development of statistics, research, experimentation and action programmes related to population.

4. Regional Cooperation in the Field of Population: 74 (XXIII)[1]

[1]Adopted unanimously 17 April 1967.

The Economic Commission for Asia and the Far East,
. . .

Noting further the resolution on dynamic Asian economic cooperation adopted at the second Ministerial Conference on Asian Economic Cooperation, held in 1965, which reiterated the vast scope for, and importance of, regional demographic cooperation,
. . .

Sharing the concern expressed in a statement signed by the Heads of State of eleven countries in 1966, which notes among other obstacles that "too rapid population growth seriously hampers efforts to raise living standards, to further education, to improve health and sanitation, to provide better housing and transportation, to forward cultural and recreational opportunities — and even in some countries to assure sufficient food,"

Expressing its appreciation of the intensified work of countries of the region and of the ECAFE secretariat in the field of population,

Noting with approval the recommendations of the Expert Working Group on the Feasibility of Establishing a Regional Population Centre, particularly those pertaining to the expansion of work on regional cooperation in the field of population through the strengthening of the ECAFE secretariat and the development of a multi-disciplinary approach,

Reiterating the increasingly urgent need for closer regional and appropriate sub-regional cooperation among countries of the ECAFE region in respect of programmes in the population field,

Emphasizing the role of the Commission in assisting Governments to improve the well-being of their peoples through development plans and programmes,

Recognizing that those efforts must take account of the interaction between population and economic and social factors in development,

Decides to establish the Asian Population Conference as a statutory organ of the Commission, to be convened every ten years synchronizing with the decennial population and related censuses, for the consideration of all aspects of population questions and of their impact on economic and social development;

Requests the Executive Secretary:

(a) To take appropriate steps to expand the regional population programme substantially as recommended by the Expert Working Group referred to above, with a view to providing for the analysis and consideration in depth of the region's population problems and for the application of the most effective means of solving them through regional and national cooperative effort;

(b) To assign primary emphasis to existing priority areas and to emerging needs of Governments for assistance in the field of population through an expanded programme of training, research, information and advisory services, making full and economical use of regional and national resources;

(c) To initiate preparations as soon as possible for the Asian Population Conference to be convened towards 1970;

Further requests the Executive Secretary to carry out for consideration by the Asian Population Conference a series of studies in depth, through secretariat research and working groups to be convened from time to time, to explore the effect of the pressure of population in delaying the achievement of development goals, and to consider the setting of targets designed to bring rates of population increase and of economic growth and social advancement into some reasonable alignment with one another in order to guide the region in attaining its growth and welfare objectives, and to provide such guidelines as may be appropriate to the implementation of the expanded programme in the field of population;

Invites the interested specialized agencies, within their respective mandates, to undertake a role commensurate with the importance of co-operative action in planning and implementing the programme, including the provision of experts, where appropriate, to participate in multi-disciplinary projects;

Calls upon all member and associate member countries of ECAFE, other members of the United Nations which are interested in the solution of population problems, and other appropriate international, regional and national institutions to extend all possible cooperation and support in implementing the expanded regional population programme.

5. Population in Relation to Economic and Social Development: III (XXVI)[1]

The Economic Commission for Asia and the Far East,
. . .

Noting with satisfaction the initiation by the secretariat of an intensified programme of work that brings regional experience and cooperation to bear on national population problems through projects that include a wide range of action-oriented studies and research, provision of training and advisory services and the establishment of a regional clearing house,

Recognizing that the growing efforts to improve the quality of life through long-term economic and social development may be frustrated by the continuance of the present high rates of population growth within the region,

1. *Calls on* member countries, in accordance with their national policies and special needs, to adopt practical and effective family planning measures on a voluntary basis aimed at the achievement of more desirable rates of population growth; and proposes that this be included

---

[1]Adopted without a vote, 24 April 1970.

among the essential aspects of the international development strategy for the Second United Nations Development Decade, looking to the eventual achievement of satisfactory *per capita* economic growth which would promote human welfare;

2. *Invites* the Administrator of the United Nations Development Programme, in allocating its resources and those of the United Nations Fund for Population Activities, to attach importance to collaborative efforts in the field of population at the regional, sub-regional and national levels, through which ECAFE cooperates in the application of the combined skills and knowledge of several agencies within the United Nations system;

3. *Endorses* the Asian Population Programme as an instrument through which the Executive Secretary can take prompt action to assist Governments to achieve their development goals.

C.   Economic Commission for Latin America (ECLA)

1.   Terms of Reference[1]

1. The Economic Commission for Latin America, acting within the framework of the policies of the United Nations and subject to the general supervision of the Council, shall, provided that the Commission takes no action in respect to any country without the agreement of the Government of that country:

(a) Initiate and participate in measures for facilitating concerted action for dealing with urgent economic problems arising out of the war and for raising the level of economic activity in Latin America and for maintaining and strengthening the economic relations of the Latin American countries both among themselves and with other countries of the world;

(b) Make or sponsor such investigations and studies of economic and technological problems and development within territories of Latin America as the Commission deems appropriate;

(c) Undertake or sponsor the collection, evaluation and dissemination of such economic, technological and statistical information as the Commission deems appropriate;

(d) Give special attention in its activities to the problems of economic development and assist in the formulation and development of coordinated policies as a basis for practical action in promoting economic development in the region;

(e) Assist the Economic and Social Council and its Technical Assistance Committee in discharging their functions with respect to the United

---

[1]As adopted by the Economic and Social Council at its sixth session and amended at its ninth, thirteenth and twenty-eighth sessions.

Nations technical assistance programme, in particular by assisting in their appraisal of these activities in the Latin American region;

(f) In carrying out the above functions, deal as appropriate with the social aspects' of economic development and the interrelationship of the economic and social factors.

. . .

(5) The Commission is empowered to make recommendations on any matters within its competence directly to the Governments of members or associate members concerned, Governments admitted in a consultative capacity, and the specialized agencies concerned. The Commission shall submit for the Council's prior consideration any of its proposals for activities that would have important effects on the economy of the world as a whole.

. . .

2. POPULATION PROBLEMS: 187 (IX)[1]

The Economic Commission for Latin America,

Considering that the factors relating to population change, structure, redistribution and characteristics have frequent and complex repercussions on economic and social development, and that demographic studies made a substantial contribution to the body of information required for formulating economic and social development programmes,

Expressing its satisfaction at the work carried out by the Population Commission and the Population Branch of the United Nations in the field of demography, and at the co-operation established between the ECLA secretariat and the Latin American Demographic Research and Training Centre in respect of studies and assistance to Governments in that field,

Decides:

1. To recommend that the regional demographic programme of the United Nations be intensified, if possible with the help of supplementary sources, so as to cater effectively for the needs of demographic research with a view to the preparation of economic and social development programmes in Latin America;

2. To request the secretariat:

(a) To pursue and intensify, in co-operation with the Latin American Demographic Research and Training Centre, a programme of studies and assistance to Governments, giving priority to the most advantageous use of the findings of the new population censuses in the formulation of economic and social development policies, and promoting the preparation of population case studies;

---

[1]Adopted unanimously 13 May 1961.

(b) That in such a programme, until detailed tabulations of the new censuses are to hand, a substantial part of the resources available be provisionally allocated to the study of the establishment of concepts and methods of analysis, especially in relation to the redistribution of the population among cities, towns and rural areas, internal migration, size and characteristics of the labour force, and its possible trends;

(c) That at future sessions of this Commission, reports on the progress made and on demographic research of importance for economic and social policy be submitted to it for consideration.

3. THE DEVELOPMENT OF LATIN AMERICA IN THE SECOND UNITED NATIONS DEVELOPMENT DECADE: 290 (XIII)[1]

The Economic Commission for Latin America,

Having taken note of the efforts the Latin American countries have been making to remove the obstacles to development,

Considering that, despite the headway made by most of the Latin American countries in some aspects of development, serious problems continue to prevent an acceleration of economic and social progress,

Bearing in mind that the Latin American countries have reaffirmed the principle that their development depends essentially on their own efforts,

Considering that, if the Latin American Governments are to devise and implement policies that will enable them to accelerate economic growth and social progress and achieve self-sustaining development in the nineteen-seventies, it will be necessary to make a more searching analysis of economic and social questions in order to provide criteria on the basis of which the Governments can select the strategies and alternatives best suited to the various types of economic policy, structure, development and social situation,

. . .

1. *Recommends* that the secretariat, in the context of its programme of work, should give special attention to studies, research and advisory services designed for:

(a) The promotion of cooperation with the Latin American Governments and the regional and sub-regional economic integration bodies in carrying out the necessary studies and furnishing any cooperation and advisory assistance the Governments may require;

. . .

(h) The study of national policies for regional development that are compatible with the aim of accelerating over-all growth, taking into ac-

---

[1]Adopted unanimously 21 April 1969.

count the problems of population concentration in urban areas and the decentralization of industrial development;

. . .

(l) The continuation of demographic studies in order to shed more light on population problems;

(m) The continuation of studies on the social and economic structure and its relationship to the development process, with special emphasis on problems which are hampering development;

(n) The improvement of statistics and data-collection, data-processing and computer services, for which purpose it is recommended that the secretariat should carry out studies and take steps to modernize its services;

. . .

4. INTERNATIONAL DEVELOPMENT STRATEGY: 310 (XIV)[1]

The Economic Commission for Latin America,

Having taken note of General Assembly resolution 2626 (XXV) laying down the International Development Strategy for the Second United Nations Development Decade, and of the document on the same subject presented by the secretariat (E/CN.12/869),

Bearing in mind that Latin America as a whole main-ained the same growth rate in the First United Nations Development Decade as in the 1950s and made significant progress in various important economic spheres, but such progress was not evenly spread over all the countries of the region, the trends were not sustained and, in general, were not reflected in qualitative and structural changes that would help to satisfy the expectations awakened or alleviate the economic and social tensions prevailing in many countries of the region,

. . .

Recognizing that the Latin American countries are anxious to attain appreciably higher development goals than in the past and to spread the resulting benefits more equitably, and that they have expressed their will and determination to participate actively in the action laid down in the United Nations International Development Strategy, inasmuch as it provides an appropriate framework for combining and harmonizing national policies and external cooperation measures,

. . .

Taking into account that the developing countries will, as appropriate, establish or strengthen their planning mechanisms, including statistical services, for formulating and implementing their national development plans during the Decade,

---

[1]Adopted unanimously 7 May 1971.

1. *Recommends* that the Governments of the developing countries members of the Commission should:

(a) Define as soon as possible their economic and social development goals and objectives in the context of their national programmes for the present decade, as indicated in the International Strategy, particularly with respect to the acceleration of their economic growth rates and the qualitative and structural changes that should accompany it, import and export needs, the mobilization of domestic resources and their complementary requirements in terms of external financial and technical cooperation;

(b) Strengthen and perfect planning systems that are attuned to each country's special characteristics, so as to provide themselves with the best possible technical bases for formulating and implementing their economic and social policies and to facilitate appraisals thereof;

(c) Adopt the necessary measures to improve their statistical services and, in particular, to make available up-to-date basic data for the periodical review and appraisal of progress towards national and regional development. These data should relate to: (i) the rate and steadiness of growth; (ii) the structural and technological changes that have occurred in the process of development; (iii) the social impact of the development process; (iv) trends and changes in the external sector.

(d) Make available periodically on a regular basis, particularly for the appraisal of the social effects of development, the basic statistical data required for following trends in: (i) employment and the structure of employment; (ii) income distribution; (iii) the level of living of the urban and rural population; (iv) regional imbalances; (v) the position with regard to nutrition, health, education, housing and other social factors;

(e) In the different international forums, press for the implementation of the policy measures contained in the International Development Strategy, both by the industrialized and by the developing countries;

. . .

5. WORLD POPULATION CONFERENCE: 327 (XV)[1]

The Economic Commission for Latin America,

Taking into account resolution 1672 (LII) dated 2 June 1972 of the Economic and Social Council on Population and Development, which, *inter alia,* recapitulates earlier resolutions of ECOSOC and the General Assembly on the resignation of 1974 as World Population Year and the holding in 1974 of a World Population Conference, makes certain recommendations on these questions, and invites the regional economic com-

---

[1]Adopted 30 March 1973.

missions to continue their population work programme in conformity with regional needs,

Taking note with satisfaction of document E/CN.12/956 submitted by the Secretariat, containing its proposals for the orientation of future work on population and for participation in the World Population Year and World Population Conference, and also of document E/CN.12/950 submitted by the Latin American Demographic Centre (CELADE), reporting on its activities and future work programmes,

Aware of the importance of continuing research into demographic trends and of objective exploration of the relationships between population and development as requisites for the formulation of population policies adapted to the circumstances and development strategies of the Latin American countries,

Considering that the Commission had adopted resolution 304 (XIV) which recognizes the Latin American Demographic Centre (CELADE) as an autonomous agency under the aegis of ECLA and requests it to continue to extend and improve its teaching and research activities and provide advisory services to the countries of the region on request,

1. *Approves* in principle the secretariat's and CELADE's proposals for the strengthening of basic demographic information and research;

2. *Urges* that the secretariat strengthen its capacity to satisfy Government requests for technical assistance in the improvement of demographic statistics and in the inclusion of demographic variables in development planning;

3. *Welcomes* the contributions of the United Nations Fund for Population Activities to the strengthening of ECLA population activities and hopes that the proposed expansion of these activities will receive favourable consideration from the Fund;

4. *Recognizes* the need for continuation of CELADE's activities in demographic research and training as an essential complement to the secretariat's programme;

5. *Urges* Member Governments to consider the possibility of continuing or expanding financial support to CELADE beyond 1974, and supports CELADE's efforts to obtain financial backing from other sources;

6. *Supports* the secretariat's participation in preparatory work for the World Population Conference and World Population Year;

7. *Recognizes* that active participation by member Governments in providing information and clarifying their own policy orientation would contribute to the success of the World Population Conference and the World Population Year;

8. *Receives* favourably the proposal for a meeting of Government representatives in early 1974 prior to the World Population Conference for the purpose of discussing the positions of the Latin American Govern-

ments in relation to the questions that will be presented to the Conference, so that the circumstances of the countries of the region and their development strategies are taken into account;

9. *Notes with satisfaction* the offer by the Government of Costa Rica to act as host for the preparatory meeting of the Latin American countries on the World Population Conference of 1974.

D. ECONOMIC COMMISSION FOR AFRICA (ECA)

1. TERMS OF REFERENCE[1]

1. The Economic Commission for Africa, acting within the framework of the policies of the United Nations and subject to the general supervision of the Economic and Social Council, shall, provided that the Commission takes no action with respect to any country without the agreement of the Government of that country:

(a) Initiate and participate in measures for facilitating concerted action for the economic development of Africa, including its social aspects, with a view to raising the level of economic activity and levels of living in Africa, and for maintaining and strengthening the economic relations of countries and territories of Africa, both among themselves and with other countries of the world;

(b) Make or sponsor such investigations and studies of economic and technological problems and developments within the territories of Africa as the Commission deems appropriate, and disseminate the results of such investigations and studies;

(c) Undertake or sponsor the collection, evaluation and dissemination of such economic, technological and statistical information as the Commission deems appropriate;

(d) Perform, within the available resources of its secretariat, such advisory services as the countries and territories of the region may desire, provided that such services do not overlap with those rendered by other bodies of the United Nations or by specialized agencies;

(e) Assist the Council at its request in discharging its functions within the region in connexion with any economic problems, including problems in the field of technical assistance;

(f) Assist in the formulation and development of coordinated policies as a basis for practical action in promoting economic and technological development in the region;

---

[1]As adopted by the Economic and Social Council, resolution 671 A (XXV), of 29 April 1958 and amended by resolution 974 D (XXVI) of 5 July 1963 and by resolution 1343 (XLV) of 18 July 1968.

(g) In carrying out the above functions, deal as appropriate with the social aspects of economic development and the interrelationship of economic and social factors.

2. The Commission is empowered to make recommendations on any matter within its competence directly to the Governments of the members or associate members concerned, to Governments admitted in a consultative capacity, and to the specialized agencies. The Commission shall submit for prior consideration by the Economic and Social Council any of its proposals for activities that would have important effects on the economy of the world as whole.

. . .

2. POPULATION: 230 (X)[1]

The Conference of Ministers,

Noting with satisfaction the work of the secretariat in demographic training,

Satisfied with the establishment within the secretariat of a Population Programme Centre,

1. *Invites* the Executive Secretary to speed up the establishment of sub-regional centres for the training of demographers;

2. *Request* the Executive Secretary, as part of the Commission's work programme, to carry out a study of population levels and trends in relation to economic and social development;

3. *Further request* the Executive Secretary, as part of the Commission's work programme, to prepare a demographic manual, which will contain concepts and definitions suitable for African countries.

E. ECONOMIC COMMISSION FOR WESTERN ASIA
TERMS OF REFERENCE[2]

The Economic and Social Council,

Recognizing the special role of the regional economic commission in the implementation of the International Development Strategy for the Second United Nations Development Decade,

Bearing in mind that the countries of Western Asia at present covered by the United Nations Economic and Social Office in Beirut do not enjoy membership in any regional economic commission,

Believing that such membership would be an important factor in accelerating their economic and social development,

---

[1] Adopted unanimously 13 February 1971.

[2] As adopted by the Economic and Social Council resolution 1818 (LV) of 9 August 1973.

Establishes an Economic Commission for Western Asia, to start its operations on 1 January 1974, with terms of reference as follows:

1. The Economic Commission for Western Asia, acting within the framework of the policies of the United Nations and subject to the general supervision of the Economic and Social Council, shall, provided that the Commission takes no action in respect of any country without the agreement of the Government of that country:

(a) Initiate and participate in measures for facilitating concerted action for the economic reconstruction and development of Western Asia, for raising the level of economic activity in Western Asia and for maintaining and strengthening the economic relations of the countries of that area both among themselves and with other countries of the world;

(b) Make or sponsor such investigations and studies of economic and technological problems and developments within the territories of Western Asia as the Commission deems appropriate;

(c) Undertake or sponsor the collection, evaluation and dissemination of such economic, technological and statistical information as the Commission deems appropriate;

(d) Perform such advisory services, within the available resources of its secretariat, as the countries of the region may desire, provided that such services do not overlap with those rendered by the specialized agencies or the United Nations Development Programme;

(e) Assist the Council, at its request, in discharging its functions within the region in connexion with any economic problems, including problems in the field of technical assistance;

(f) In carrying out the above functions, deal, as appropriate, with the social aspects of economic development and the interrelationship of the economic and social factors.

2. The members of the Commission shall consist of the States Members of the United Nations situated in Western Asia which at present call on the services of the United Nations Economic and Social Office in Beirut. Future applications for membership by Member States shall be decided on by the Council upon the recommendation of the Commission.

3. The Commission is empowered to make recommendations on any matters within its competence directly to the Governments of members concerned, Governments admitted in consultative capacity and the specialized agencies concerned. The Commission shall submit for the Council's prior consideration any of its proposals for activities that would have important effects on the economy of the world as a whole.

. . .

PART SIX

OTHER UNITED NATIONS BODIES

PART VI.
OTHER UNITED NATIONS BODIES[1]

A. UNITED NATIONS CONFERENCE ON TRADE AND DEVELOPMENT (UNCTAD)[2]

The General Assembly,

Convinced that sustained efforts are necessary to raise the standards of living in all countries and to accelerate the economic growth of the developing countries,

Considering that international trade is an important instrument for economic development,

Recognizing that the United Nations Conference on Trade and Development has provided a unique opportunity to make a comprehensive review of the problems of trade and of trade in relation to economic development, particularly those problems affecting the developing countries,

Convinced that adequate and effectively functioning organizational arrangements are essential if the full contribution of international trade to the accelerated economic growth of the developing countries is to be successfully realized through the formulation and implementation of the necessary policies,

. . .

I

Establishes the United Nations Conference on Trade and Development as an organ of the General Assembly in accordance with the provisions set forth in section II below;

II

. . .

3. The principal functions of the Conference shall be:

(a) To promote international trade, especially with a view to accelerating economic development, particularly trade between countries at different stages of development, between developing countries and between countries with different systems of economic and social organization, taking into account the functions performed by existing international organizations;

---

[1]Unless otherwise indicated the resolutions quoted in this section are resolutions of the General Assembly.

[2]Adopted without objection, 30 December 1964.

(b) To formulate principles and policies on international trade and related problems of economic development;

(c) To make proposals for putting the said principles and policies into effect and to take such other steps within its competence as may be relevant to this end, having regard to differences in economic systems and stages of development;

. . .

B.   United Nations Industrial Development Organization (UNIDO)[1]

The General Assembly,

Recognizing that the industrialization of developing countries is essential for their economic and social development and for the expansion and diversification of their trade,

Conscious of the fact that the acceleration of industrial development, especially in the developing countries, depends largely on the broadest international cooperation,

Considering the widespread desire for a comprehensive organization capable of intensifying, coordinating and expediting the efforts of the United Nations system in the field of industrial development,

Bearing in mind the need for special measures designed to give additional impetus to the industrialization of the less advanced of the developing countries,

Recalling its resolution 2089 (XX) of 20 December 1965, by which it established within the United Nations an autonomous organization for the promotion of industrial development,

. . .

I

Decides that the United Nations Industrial Development Organization (hereinafter referred to as the Organization), established as an organ of the General Assembly, shall function as an autonomous organization within the United Nations in accordance with the provisions set forth in section II below;

II

Purpose

1. The purpose of the Organization shall be to promote industrial development, in accordance with Article 1, paragraph 3, and Articles 55

---

[1]Adopted by 109 votes to none, with no abstentions, 17 November 1966.

and 56 of the Charter of the United Nations, and by encouraging the mobilization of national and international resources to assist in, promote and accelerate the industrialization of the developing countries, with particular emphasis on the manufacturing sector.

Functions

2. In the fulfilment of its purpose, the Organization shall undertake:
(a) Operational activities, including in particular:

(i) Encouragement and promotion of and making of recommendations for national, regional and international action to achieve more rapid industrialization of developing countries;

(ii) Contribution to the most effective application in the developing countries of modern industrial methods of production, programming and planning, taking into account the experience of States with different social and economic systems;

(iii) Building and strengthening of institutions and administration in the developing countries in the matter of industrial technology, production, programming and planning;

(iv) Dissemination of information on technological innovations originating in various countries and, for the developing countries, assistance in the implementation of practical measures for the application of such information, the adaptation of existing technology and the development of new technology especially suited to the particular physical, social and economic conditions of developing countries through the establishment and improvement, *inter alia*, of technological research centres in these countries;

(v) Assistance, at the request of Governments of developing countries, in the formulation of industrial development programmes and in the preparation of specific industrial projects, including, as necessary, technical and economic feasibility studies;

. . .

(b) Action-oriented studies and research programmes designed especially to facilitate the activities outlined in sub-paragraph (a) above, including in particular the compilation, analysis, publication and dissemination of information concerning various aspects of the process of industrialization, such as industrial technology, investment, financing, production, management techniques, programming and planning.

. . .

C. UNITED NATIONS CHILDREN'S FUND (UNICEF)

1. ESTABLISHMENT OF AN INTERNATIONAL CHILDREN'S EMERGENCY FUND:57 (I)[1]

The General Assembly,

Having considered the resolution adopted by the Economic and Social Council at its third session recommending the creation of an International Children's Emergency Fund to be utilized for the benefit of children and adolescents of countries which were the victims of aggression, and recognizing the desirability of establishing such a Fund in accordance with Article 55 of the Charter of the United Nations,

Decides, therefore:

1. There is hereby created an International Children's Emergency Fund to be utilized and administered, to the extent of its available resources:

(a) For the benefit of children and adolescents of countries which were victims of aggression and in order to assist in their rehabilitation;

(b) For the benefit of children and adolescents of countries at present receiving assistance from the United Nations Relief and Rehabilitation Administration;

(c) For child health purposes generally, giving high priority to the children of countries victims of aggression.

. . .

(b) The Fund, in agreement with the Governments concerned, shall take such measures as are deemed appropriate to ensure the proper utilization and distribution of supplies or other assistance which it provides. Supplies or other assistance shall be made available to Governments upon approval by the Fund of the plans of operation drawn up by the Governments concerned. Provision shall be made for:

(i) The submission to the Fund of such reports on the use of supplies and other assistance as the Fund may from time to time require;

(ii) Equitable and efficient dispensation or distribution of all supplies or other assistance, on the basis of need, without discrimination because of race, creed, nationality status or political belief;

(c) The Fund shall not engage in activity in any country except in consultation with, and with the consent of, the Government concerned;

. . .

---

[1]Adopted unanimously 11 December 1946.

2. Continuing Needs of Children: United Nations
   International Children's Emergency Fund:417 (V)[1]

The General Assembly,

. . .

Recognizing the necessity for continued action to relieve the sufferings of children, particularly in under-developed countries and countries that have been subjected to the devastation of war and to other calamities,

1. *Reaffirms* its approval of the policy of the Executive Board of the United Nations International Children's Emergency Fund to devote a greater share of the Fund's resources to the development of programmes outside Europe;

. . .

5. *Requests* the Economic and Social Council, in consultation with the appropriate specialized agencies:

(a) To give greater emphasis to support of national programmes designed to aid children within the framework of existing United Nations activities for promoting the economic and social development of under-developed areas;

(b) To explore the means of procuring and financing supplies incidental to such programmes, especially those needed for demonstration purposes;

. . .

3. United Nations Children's Fund (UNICEF):802 (VIII)[2]

The General Assembly,

Considering the world-wide disproportion between the magnitude of social service tasks to be undertaken and the available means of implementation,

Considering the role that the United Nations International Children's Emergency Fund plays in the whole international programme for the protection of the child,

Considering that the Fund's activities are useful, not only because they realize some of the high objectives which have been adopted by the United Nations, but also because they create favourable conditions for the development of the long-range economic and social programmes of the United Nations and the specialized agencies, particularly the World

---

[1]Adopted unanimously 1 December 1950.

[2]Adopted unanimously 6 October 1953.

Health Organization and the Food and Agriculture Organization of the United Nations,

Considering the urgent need for continuing the work of UNICEF, particularly in the under-developed regions of the world,

Considering that the number of Governments making contributions to UNICEF has increased constantly since 1950,

1. *Affirms* that the regulations which govern the activity of the United Nations International Children's Emergency Fund have enabled it to achieve satisfactory techniques, to acquire valuable experience and to accomplish its task successfully;

2. *Reaffirms* the pertinent provisions of General Assembly resolutions 57 (I) and 417 (V), with the exception of any reference to time-limits contained in these resolutions;

3. *Decides* to change the name of the organization to the *United Nations Children's Fund*, retaining the symbol UNICEF;

4. *Requests* the Economic and Social Council to continue to review periodically the work of UNICEF and to make recommendations to the General Assembly as appropriate;

5. *Requests* the Secretary-General:

(a) To ensure that the programmes carried on by UNICEF continue to be coordinated effectively with the regular and technical assistance programmes of the United Nations and the specialized agencies;

. . .

4. POSSIBLE ROLE OF UNICEF IN FAMILY PLANNING PROGRAMMES: UNICEF EXECUTIVE BOARD RESOLUTION[1]

The Executive Board,

. . .

Taking into account the points of view expressed by members of the Executive Board in their discussion on this subject,

1. *Expresses* its appreciation to the Executive Director for his report;

2. *Decides* to defer action on the recommendations of the Executive Director until the 1967 session of the Board;

3. *Requests* the advice of the UNICEF/WHO Joint Committee on Health Policy on the best way in which UNICEF might participate in programmes of family planning, with particular reference to the technical aspects; in so doing the Executive Board requests the UNICEF members of the Joint Committee on Health Policy to be guided by the following principles:

(a) UNICEF assistance shall be given in response to Government re-

---

[1]E/ICEF/CRP/66-43. Adopted 6 October 1966 with no objection.

quests, as part of a country's health services and not as a separate category of assistance;

(b) UNICEF assistance shall be limited to the usual forms of aid that have been approved by the Executive Board for many years, such as training of personnel, provision of vehicles, and supplies and equipment for maternal and child health services;

(c) UNICEF shall not take any responsibility for the organization and administration of the governmental programme relating to family planning;

(d) UNICEF shall request the technical advice of WHO and the Bureau of Social Affairs of the United Nations Secretariat in connexion with any such assistance.

. . .

5. HEALTH ASPECTS OF FAMILY PLANNING:
   UNICEF EXECUTIVE BOARD DECISION

[Conclusions of the UNICEF/WHO Joint Committee on Health Policy (Fifteenth Session) as approved by the UNICEF Executive Board at its June 1967 session.][1]

"The types of projects in family planning for which a country might request UNICEF/WHO assistance and which, if they meet the requirements outlined" [in the Joint Committee on Health Policy Report], "could receive WHO technical approval would be those directed at (1) training in MCH care including family planning for the health personnel, (2) the expansion of the basic health services including the maternal and child health services. The need for rapid expansion of health services to provide scope for family planning as an integral part of them should be recognized. The normal preventive and curative activities of those services should in no way be reduced or impaired."

D. UNITED NATIONS FUND FOR POPULATION ACTIVITIES (UNFPA)

1. GENERAL ASSEMBLY RESOLUTION 2815 (XXVI)[2]
   UNITED NATIONS FUND FOR POPULATION ACTIVITIES

The General Assembly,

Recalling Economic and Social Council resolution 1084 (XXXIX) of 30 July 1965 on the work programmes and priorities in the population fields,

---

[1]E/ICEF/556 at pp. 13-15, and 563 at para. 58, p. 18 (1967).

[2]Adopted by 94 votes to none, with 20 abstentions, 14 December 1971.

Recalling further its resolution 2211 (XXI) of 17 December 1966, in response to which a trust fund, subsequently named the United Nations Fund for Population Activities, was established in 1967 by the Secretary-General,

Bearing in mind the International Development Strategy for the Second United Nations Development Decade contained in General Assembly resolution 2626 (XXV) of 24 October 1970, with particular reference to the demographic objectives and policy measures set forth in paragraphs 13 and 65 of the Strategy,

Recognizing the responsibility of the Population Commission to assist the Economic and Social Council in accordance with its terms of reference, as defined in Economic and Social Council resolution 150 (VII) of 10 August 1948,

Noting that the Secretary-General has requested the Administrator of the United Nations Development Programme to administer the United Nations Fund for Population Activities and that an Executive Director for the Fund has been appointed,

Further noting wtih satisfaction the progress made to date by the United Nations Fund for Population Activities to which, so far, 32 countries have contributed,

Aware that the United Nations Fund for Population Activities has now been a viable entity in the United Nations system,

Convinced that the United Nations Fund for Population Activities should play a leading role in the United Nations system in promoting population programmes consistent with the decisions of the General Assembly and the Economic and Social Council, on the problem of fast population growth as well as on the problem of under-population, which could, among other things, hamper rapid economic development,

Recognizing the need for the executing agencies of the United Nations Fund for Population Activities to implement with dispatch, in close cooperation with the Fund, population programmes requested by developing countries in order that such programmes may have the desired impact,

Expressing its appreciation of the efforts of the Secretary-General, which have resulted in the unprecedented growth and expansion of the Fund, and of the support extended by the Administrator of the United Nations Development Programme,

1. *Invites* Governments which are in a position to do so and whose policies would allow it to make voluntary contributions to the Fund;

2. *Requests* the Secretary-General, in consultation with the Administrator of the United Nations Development Programme and the Executive Director of the United Nations Fund for Population Activities, to take the necessary steps to achieve the desired improvements in the administrative machinery of the Fund aimed at the efficient and expeditious deliv-

ery of population programmes, including measures to quicken the pace of recruiting the experts and personnel required to cope with the increasing volume of requests, as well as to consider the training of experts and personnel in the developing countires;

3. *Further requests* the Secretary-General to inform the Economic and Social Council at its fifty-third session and the General Assembly at its twenty-seventh session of the steps he has taken in the implementation of the present resolution and of any recommendations he may wish to make in this regard.

2. GENERAL ASSEMBLY RESOLUTION 3019 (XXVII)
    UNITED NATIONS FUND FOR POPULATION ACTIVITIES[1]

The General Assembly,
. . .

Welcoming the Secretary-General's note with interim recommendations requiring urgent action to achieve improvements in the administrative machinery of the United Nations Fund for Population Activities aimed at the efficient and expeditious delivery of population programmes,

Expressing its appreciation to the 52 Member States which, to date, have responded to that invitation and have pledged financial support to the United Nations Fund for Population Activities,

Noting the advice from the Secretary-General that the administration of the United Nations Fund for Population Activities has been reorganized over the past year in order to make even more effective use of its staff and resources,

Noting further that the resources of the United Nations Fund for Population Activities and its scope of operations have now grown to a size which makes its supervision by an intergovernmental body desirable,

Expressing further its appreciation to the Administrator of the United Nations Development Programme and to the Executive Director of the United Nations Fund for Population Activities for their efforts which have achieved the significant results of the past year,

Noting also the recommendation of the Secretary-General to change the character of the United Nations Fund for Population Activities from a trust fund of the Secretary-General into a fund established under the authority of the General Assembly,

1. *Decides* to place the United Nations Fund for Population Activities under the authority of the General Assembly;

2. *Decides further,* without prejudice to the over-all responsibilities and policy functions of the Economic and Social Council, that the Gov-

---

[1]Adopted by 106 votes to none, with 20 abstentions, 18 December 1972.

erning Council of the United Nations Development Programme, subject to conditions to be established by the Economic and Social Council, shall be the governing body of the United Nations Fund for Population Activities and invites the Governing Council to concern itself with the financial and administrative policies concerning the work programme, the fund-raising methods and the annual budget of the Fund;

3. *Invites* the Governing Council to organize itself in such a way that it can exercise effectively these functions, taking into account the separate identify of the United Nations Fund for Population Activities and its need to operate under the guidance of the Economic and Social Council, in close relationship with interested Governments and with appropriate international and national bodies governmental and non-governmental, interested in population activities;

4. *Authorizes* the Governing Council, at its fifteenth session, to appoint funding principles similar to those of the United Nations Development Programme to the United Nations Fund for Population Activities and to establish the necessary financial rules and regulations, subject to consideration by the Governing Council of a report, prepared by the Executive Director of the United Nations Fund for Population Activities in consultation with the Administrator of the United Nations Development Programme, and of the full implications thereof;

5. *Requests* the Governing Council to consider further steps necessary to achieve improvements in the administrative and operational machinery of the United Nations Fund for Population Activities and to inform the Economic and Social Council in its annual report of those further steps taken to implement General Assembly resolution 2815 (XXVI) and the present resolution and to submit annually a report on the activities of the United Nations Fund for Population Activities to the Economic and Social Council;

6. *Renews* its invitation to interested Governments to make voluntary contributions to the United Nations Fund for Population Activities without prejudice to the agreed level of growth of contributions to the United Nations Development Programme and developmental assistance in general.

3. Decision of the UNDP Governing Council (XV) (1973)[1]

The Governing Council:

. . .

(b) *Authorized* the Executive Director of UNFPA:

(i) To continue to conduct the financial operations of the Fund on a provisional basis under the appropriate Financial Regulations and

---
[1]Adopted without a vote, 7 February 1973 (365th meeting).

Rules of UNDP, taking into account the separate identity and character of the Fund;

(ii) To depart from a system of full funding and establish on a provisional basis an operational reserve of $20 million;

(iii) To allocate funds, in accordance with Regulation 12.1 of the UNDP Financial Regulations and Rules and pending consideration at its sixteenth session of revised estimates of UNFPA resources and programme costs for the period 1973-1976, up to the level of $26 million to carry out new UNFPA activities.

(c) *Requested* the Executive Director of UNFPA to submit to the sixteenth session of the Governing Council:

(i) A detailed report, including administrative budget estimates for the UNFPA Secretariat and information on firm pledges received for 1973, taking into account the views expressed in the Budgetary and Finance Committee as well as the views expressed in the Economic and Social Council at its fifty-fourth session, which would allow the Council to take appropriate action in conformity with General Assembly resolution 3019 (XXVII);

(ii) A work plan as well as a revised statement showing any further adjustments in the estimates of annual programme costs for the period 1973-1976;

(iii) Draft financial regulations and rules for the Fund;

(d) *Invited* the Executive Director of UNFPA to study the various possible means of regularizing pledging procedures in the light of observations made in the Budgetary and Finance Committee.

4. UNITED NATIONS FUND FOR POPULATION ACTIVITIES: 1763 (LIV)[1]

The Economic and Social Council,

Recalling General Assembly resolution 2815 (XXVI) of 14 December 1971 with its requests to the Secretary-General regarding the United Nations Fund for Population Activities, and the note by the Secretary-General in response to that resolution,

Welcoming General Assembly resolution 3019 (XXVII) of 18 December 1972, which placed the United Nations Fund for Population Activities under the authority of the Governing Council of the United Nations Development Programme as the governing body, subject to the conditions to be established by the Economic and Social Council,

Bearing in mind the important work undertaken by the regional economic commissions and their specialized organs concerned with population matters,

---

[1]Adopted 18 May 1973.

Aware of the fact that there are considerable differences in the population and demographic situations in each country and that it is therefore necessary to adopt different approaches and solutions for each country,

Expressing its desire that the Fund, in the elaboration of its plans and programmes, should take into account the resolutions adopted by the regional economic commissions and their specialized organs dealing with population matters,

Reiterating the importance of maintaining the separate identity of the United Nations Fund for Population Activities under the general arrangements provided for in General Assembly resolution 3019 (XXVII),

Recalling the willingness with which the Governing Council of the United Nations Development Programme and the Administrator of the Programme assumed their responsibilities in regard to the Fund,

Noting the report of the Executive Director of the United Nations Fund for Population Activities,

Noting further in the annex to the report the recommendations to the Secretary-General from the Review Committee of the United Nations Fund for Population Activities,

Expressing its appreciation for the initiative and leadership which has characterized the development of the Fund,

Mindful that in taking action on this resolution the Council is fully cognizant of the fact that the World Population Conference will mark new development in population policy for the world community of nations and for the population activities of the United Nations system,

1. *States* that the aims and purposes of the United Nations Fund for Population Activities are:

(a) To build up, on an international basis, with the assistance of the competent bodies of the United Nations system, the knowledge and the capacity to respond to national, regional, interregional and global needs in the population and family planning fields; to promote co-ordination in planning and programming, and to co-operate with all concerned;

(b) To promote awareness, both in developed and in developing countries, of the social, economic and environmental implications of national and international population problems; of the human rights aspects of family planning; and of possible strategies to deal with them, in accordance with the plans and priorities of each country;

(c) To extend systematic and sustained assistance to developing countries at their request in dealing with their population; such assistance to be afforded in forms and by means requested by the recipient countries and best suited to meet the individual country's needs;

(d) To play a leading role in the United Nations system in promoting population programmes and to co-ordinate projects supported by the Fund;

2. *Decides* that the United Nations Fund for Population Activities should invite countries to utilize the most appropriate implementing agents for their programmes, recognizing that the primary responsibility for implementing rests with the countries concerned;

3. *Requests* the Governing Council of the United Nations Development Programme to submit annually to the Economic and Social Council a report on the activities of the United Nations Fund for Population Activities.

PART SEVEN

THE SPECIALIZED AGENCIES

A. International Labour Organisation (ILO)

1. Constitution[1]

Preamble

Whereas universal and lasting peace can be established only if it is based upon social justice;

And whereas conditions of labour exist involving such injustice, hardship and privation to large numbers of people as to produce unrest so great that the peace and harmony of the world are imperilled; and an improvement of those conditions is urgently required: as, for example, by the regulation of the hours of work, including the establishment of a maximum working day and week, the regulation of the labour supply, the prevention of unemployment, the provision of an adequate living wage, the protection of the worker against sickness, disease and injury arising out of his employment, the protection of children, young persons and women, provision for old age and injury, protection of the interests of workers when employed in countries other than their own, recognition of the principle of equal remuneration for work of equal value, recognition of the principle of freedom of association, the organization of vocational and technical education and other measures;

Whereas also the failure of any nation to adopt humane conditions of labour is an obstacle in the way of other nations which desire to improve the conditions in their own countries;

The High Contracting Parties, moved by sentiments of justice and humanity as well as by the desire to secure the permanent peace of the world, and with a view to attaining the objectives set forth in this Preamble, agree to the following Constitution of the International Labour Organisation:

---

[1]The original Constitution of the International Labour Organisation was in Part XIII of the Treaty of Versailles signed on June 28, 1919, 49 Stat. 2712. The ILO was separated from the League of Nations by an amendment adopted by the International Labour Conference at Paris on November 7, 1945, 2 UNTS 17. The present Constitution originated with the Instrument for the Amendment of the Constitution of the ILO adopted by the International Labour Conference at Montreal on October 9, 1946, 15 UNTS 35. The 1946 Amendment incorporates the Declaration concerning the Aims and Purposes of the ILO, adopted by the International Labour Conference at Philadelphia, May 10, 1944, 15 UNTS 104. The Constitution was further amended in 1953 and 1962.

Article 1

1. A permanent organization is hereby established for the promotion of the objects set forth in the Preamble to this Constitution and in the Declaration concerning the aims and purposes of the International Labour Organisation adopted at Philadelphia on 10 May 1944 the text of which is annexed to this Constitution.

. . .

ANNEX

1. DECLARATION CONCERNING THE AIMS AND PURPOSES OF THE INTERNATIONAL LABOUR ORGANISATION

The General Conference of the International Labour Organisation, meeting in its Twenty-sixth Session in Philadelphia, hereby adopts, this tenth day of May in the year nineteen hundred and forty-four, the present Declaration of the aims and purposes of the International Labour Organisation and of the principles which should inspire the policy of its Members.

I

The Conference reaffirms the fundamental principles on which the Organisation is based and, in particular, that:

. . .

(c) poverty anywhere constitutes a danger to prosperity everywhere;

(d) the war against want requires to be carried on with unrelenting vigour within each nation, and by continuous and concerted international effort in which the representatives of workers and employers, enjoying equal status with those of Governments, join with them in free discussion and democratic decision with a view to the promotion of the common welfare.

II

Believing that experience has fully demonstrated the truth of the statement in the Constitution of the International Labour Organisation that lasting peace can be established only if it is based on social justice, the Conference affirms that:

(a) all human beings, irrespective of race, creed or sex, have the right to pursue both their material well-being and their spiritual development in conditions of freedom and dignity, of economic security and equal opportunity;

(b) the attainment of the conditions in which this shall be possible must constitute the central aim of national and international policy:

. . .

188

(e) in discharging the tasks entrusted to it the International Labour Organisation, having considered all relevant economic and financial factors, may include in its decisions and recommendations any provisions which it considers appropriate.

III

The Conference recognizes the solemn obligation of the International Labour Organisation to further among the nations of the world programmes which will achieve:

(a) full employment and the raising of standards of living;

(b) the employment of workers in the occupations in which they can have the satisfaction of giving the fullest measure of their skill and attainments and make their greatest contribution to the common well-being:

(c) the provision, as a means to the attainment of this end and under adequate guarantees for all concerned, of facilities for training and the transfer of labour, including migration for employment and settlement;

(d) policies in regard to wages and earnings, hours and other conditions of work calculated to ensure a just share of the fruits of progress to all, and a minimum living wage to all employed and in need of such protection;

(e) the effective recognition of the right of collective bargaining, the cooperation of management and labour in the continous improvement of productive efficiency, and the collaboration of workers and employers in the preparation and application of social and economic measures;

(f) the extension of social security measures to provide a basic income to all in need of such protection and comprehensive medical care;

(g) adequate protection for the life and health of workers in all occupations;

(h) provision for child welfare and maternity protection;

(i) the provision of adequate nutrition, housing and facilities for recreation and culture;

(j) the assurance of equality of educational and vocational opportunity.
. . .

2. Equal Remuneration Convention, 1951.
   (See under Part II above)

3. Recommendation Concerning the Protection of Migrant Workers in Undeveloped Countries and Territories[1]

The General Conference of the International Labour Organisation,
. . .

---

[1]Adopted by 161 votes to 18, with no abstentions, 22 June 1955.

adopts this twenty-second day of June of the year one thousand nine hundred and fifty-five the following Recommendation, which may be cited as the Protection of Migrant Workers (Underdeveloped Countries) Recommendation, 1955:

I. Definitions and Scope

1. This Recommendation applies to—

(a) countries and territories in which the evolution from a subsistence form of economy towards more advanced forms of economy, based on wage earning and entailing sporadic and scattered development of industrial and agricultural centres, brings with it appreciable migratory movements of workers and sometimes their families;

(b) countries and territories through which such migratory movements of workers pass on their outward and, where applicable, their return journeys, if existing arrangements in such countries and territories, taken as a whole, afford less protection to the persons concerned during their journeys than is laid down in this Recommendation;

(c) countries and territories of destination of such migratory movements of workers, if existing arrangements in such countries and territories, taken as a whole, afford less protection to the persons concerned during their journeys or employment than is laid down in this Recommendation.

. . .

III. Measures to Discourage Migratory Movements when Considered Undesirable in the Interests of the Migrant Workers and of the Communities and Countries of Their Origin

16. The general policy should be to discourage migration of workers when considered undesirable in the interests of the migrant workers and of the communities and countries of their origin by measures designed to improve conditions of life and to raise standards of living in the areas from which the migrations normally start.

17. The measures to be taken to ensure the application of the policy described in the preceding paragraph should include--

(a) in emigration areas, the adoption of economic development and vocational training programmes to enable fuller use to be made of available manpower and natural resources, and in particular the adoption of all measures likely to create new jobs and new sources of income for workers who would normally be disposed to emigrate;

(b) in immigration areas, the more rational use of manpower and the increase of productivity through better organization of work, better train-

190

ing and the development of mechanization or other measures as local circumstances may require;

(c) the limitation of recruitment in regions where the withdrawal of labour might have untoward effects on the social and economic organization, and the health, welfare and development of the population concerned.

18. The Governments of the countries and territories of origin and destination of migrant workers should endeavour to bring about a progressive reduction of migratory movements which have not been subject or appeared open to regulation, when such movements are considered undesirable in the interests of the migrant workers and of the communities and countries of their origin. So long as the economic causes of these unregulated migrations persist, the Governments concerned should endeavour to exercise appropriate control, to the extent that such action appears practicable and desirable, over voluntary migration as well as organized recruitment. Such reduction and control may be sought by means of arrangements at local or area level and through bilateral agreements.

. . .

IV. PROTECTION OF MIGRANT WORKERS DURING THE PERIOD OF THEIR EMPLOYMENT

. . .

G. Social Security, Industrial Safety and Hygiene

45. The steps to be taken for migrant workers should in any case include in the first instance appropriate arrangements, without discrimination on grounds of nationality, race or religion, for workmen's compensation, medical care for workers and their families, industrial hygiene and prevention of accidents and occupational diseases.

46. These arrangements should include--

(a) medical supervision in accordance with local possibilities by periodical visits in the course of employment, and in case of sickness;

(b) first aid, free medical treatment and hospitalization facilities in accordance with standards to be prescribed by the competent authority;

. . .

(j) special health and social measures for the protection of the migrant worker's wife and children living with him.

. . .

H. Relations of Migrant Workers with Their Areas of Origin

48. Arrangements should be made to enable migrant workers to maintain contact with their families and their areas of origin, including--

(a) the granting of such facilities as may be required for the voluntary remittance of funds to the worker's family in his area of origin or elsewhere and for the accumulation, with the assent of the worker, of deferred pay which he should receive at the end of his contract or when he returns to his home or in any other circumstances to be decided in agreement with him;

(b) facilities for the exchange of correspondence between the migrant worker, his family and his area of origin;

(c) facilities for the performance by the migrant worker of those customary obligations to his community of origin which he wishes to observe.

. . .

V. STABILIZATION OF MIGRANT WORKERS

. . .

52. (1) Where lasting settlement of migrant workers at or near their place of employment is found to be possible, arrangements should be made to promote their permanent installation.

(2) These arrangements should include--

(a) encouragement of recruitment of migrant workers accompanied by their families;

(b) the granting wherever possible and desirable of facilities to enable the establishment at or near the place of employment of appropriate community organization;

(c) the provision of housing of an approved standard and at suitable cost to promote the permanent settlement of families;

(d) the allocation, wherever possible and desirable, of sufficient land for the production of foodstuffs;

(e) in the absence of more appropriate facilities and whenever possible and desirable, the creation of villages or settlements of retired migrant workers in places where it is possible for them to contribute to their own subsistence.

. . .

4. DISCRIMINATION (EMPLOYMENT AND OCCUPATION) CONVENTION, 1958. (SEE UNDER PART II ABOVE)

5. THE INFLUENCE OF RAPID POPULATION GROWTH.[1]

The General Conference of the International Labour Organisation.

Recalling the Employment Policy Recommendation, 1964, adopted by the International Labour Conference at its 48th (1964) Session, in which it is stated that "countries in which the population is increasing rapidly,

---

[1] Adopted 29 June 1967.

and especially those in which it already presses heavily on the economy, should study the economic, social and demographic factors affecting population growth with a view to adopting economic and social policies that make for a better balance between the growth of employment opportunities and the growth of the labour force",

Bearing in mind the Conclusions of the 13th (1966) Session of the Asian Advisory Committee relating to human resources development, unanimously adopted by the Governing Body at its 168th (February-March 1967) Session, in which it is stated, *inter alia,* that "rapid population growth in many Asian countries is seriously depressing the level of income and welfare of most families and aggravating the already acute employment problems", and that countries "should consider the adoption of a population policy suited to national considerations which may be designed to reduce the rate of population growth by means of family planning",

Taking into account resolution No. 2211 (XXI) on population growth and economic development, adopted by the United Nations General Assembly on 17 December 1966, which affirms "that demographic problems require the consideration of economic, social, cultural, psychological and health factors in their proper perspective", recognizes "the sovereignty of nations in formulating and promoting their own population policies, with due regard to the principle that the size of the family should be according to the free choice of each individual family", and calls upon "the specialized agencies concerned to assist, when requested, in further developing and strengthening national and regional facilities for training, research, information and advisory services in the field of population, bearing in mind the different character of population problems in each country and region and the needs arising therefrom",

Recognizing that in many countries, in spite of considerable efforts to create more employment opportunities and promote a better utilization of human resources, unemployment and underemployment are causing increasingly serious economic and social problems including that of creating employment opportunities for young school-leavers,

Noting that these problems may be aggravated by rapid population growth and that, for this reason, a number of countries are now seeking to secure a moderate rate of population growth,

Believing that Governments as well as trade unions and employers' organizations have an important role to play in creating awareness of the implications of rapid population growth particularly in developing countries;

Invites the Governing Body of the International Labour Office to request the Director-General—

(a) to undertake a comprehensive study on the influence and consequences of rapid population growth on opportunities for training and employment and on welfare of workers, with particular reference to developing countries, and to cooperate closely towards this aim with the United Nations and with other competent international organizations, taking into account the various studies already undertaken in this field by national, regional and international institutions;

(b) to submit, in the light of such a study, proposals to the Governing Body on the further action that might be taken by the International Labour Organisation within its field of competence and in close cooperation with the United Nations and other competent national, regional or international organizations.

6. ENLARGED MANDATE FOR ACTION IN THE POPULATION FIELD, ADOPTED BY THE ILO GOVERNING BODY (1968)[1]

7. PROPOSED CONCLUSIONS OF THE COMMITTEE ON THE WORLD EMPLOYMENT PROGRAMME[2]

General Principles

1. Following the endorsement of the World Employment Programme and the unanimous adoption of the International Development Strategy for the Second Development Decade (DD2), one objective of which is "to raise substantially the level of employment", Member States should make vigorous efforts to achieve this goal by applying as speedily as possible the policies advocated in the Employment Policy Convention and Recommendation (No. 122), in the International Development Strategy and in the Consensus approved by the UNDP Governing Council on technical cooperation procedures in the UN development cycle.

2. The immediate objective of such employment policies should be to raise the standard of living of the working population as a whole.

3. In order to achieve this objective, developing countries should—

(a) adopt full, productive and freely-chosen employment as a major goal of their national development policies and formulate their employment objectives so as to reduce significantly unemployment and underemployment particularly among young people, and to absorb an increasing part of their working population in more productive activities, through sustained economic growth;

---

[1]See ILO Minutes of the 173rd Session of the Governing Body, Appendix IV, pp. 63, 66-69 (1968). The Governing Body endorsed the lines of possible ILO action to induce and help developing countries to moderate their rate of population growth in appropriate cases discussed in paragraphs 25 to 44 of the document on this agenda item submitted to it by the Director-General.

[2]Adopted by the International Labour Conference without objection, subject to reservations as to para. 4 by five member States, 23 June 1971.

(b) orient all aspects of their development policy towards full employment and take the necessary measures to overcome such obstacles to employment-oriented development policies as may exist within the structure of their economy and society;

(c) review immediately national legislation, policies and practices that may limit the employment of workers, and minimize government expenditure on prestige programmes in order to facilitate the financing of employment projects;

(d) implement agrarian reforms, as advocated in the Employment Policy Recommendation (No. 122), as a condition for the development of the rural sector and the provision of productive employment in that sector, and coordinate these with policies for a development of industry that is as diversified as possible.

4. Rapid population growth in many developing countries is giving rise to serious employment problems. Due attention should be given to the adoption, where necessary, of population policies and, in appropriate cases, to the introduction of family planning programmes. International organizations, including the ILO, should assist, as appropriate and within their field of competence, in the formulation of such policies and programmes.

. . .

B.   Food and Agriculture Organization (FAO)

1.   Constitution[1]

Preamble

The Nations accepting this Constitution, being determined to promote the common welfare by furthering separate and collective action on their part for the purposes of:

  raising levels of nutrition and standards of living of the peoples under their respective jurisdictions;

  securing improvements in the efficiency of the production and distribution of all food and agricultural products;

  bettering the condition of rural populations;

  and thus contributing toward an expanding world economy;
hereby establish the Food and Agriculture Organization of the United Nations, hereinafter referred to as the "Organization", through which the Members will report to one another on the measures taken and the progress achieved in the fields of action set forth above.

---

[1]Adopted 16 October 1945.

Functions of the Organization

1. The Organization shall collect, analyze, interpret and disseminate information relating to nutrition, food and agriculture. In this Constitution, the term "agriculture" and its derivatives include fisheries, marine products, forestry and primary forestry products.

2. The Organization shall promote and, where appropriate, shall recommend national and international action with respect to:

(a) scientific, technological, social and economic research relating to nutrition, food and agriculture;

(b) the improvement of education and administration relating to nutrition, food and agriculture, and the spread of public knowledge of nutritional and agricultural science and practice;

(c) the conservation of natural resources and the adoption of improved methods of agricultural production;

. . .

3. It shall also be the function of the Organization:

(a) to furnish such technical assistance as Governments may request;

(b) to organize, in cooperation with the Governments concerned, such missions as may be needed to assist them to fulfil the obligations arising from their acceptance of the recommendations of the United Nations Conference on Food and Agriculture and of this Constitution; and

(c) generally to take all necessary and appropriate action to implement the purposes of the Organization as set forth in the Preamble.

2. GENERAL STRUCTURE[1]

The Conference

Recognizing that the world is faced with a growing crisis in its efforts to achieve and maintain a reasonable balance between a rapidly expanding population and the food supply;

Recognizing, also, that substantial improvements must be brought about in agricultural production, processing, distribution and utilization if the needs of the developing countries are to be adequately met;

Recognizing, also, the necessity for organizations of the United Nations family in the field of economic and social cooperation to adapt their activities, and consequently their structures, to the requirements of coordinated and integrated action towards development, and in the case of FAO, also to new programmes in particular those which may result from the Indicative World Plan;

---

[1]FAO Conference resolution No. 1/67, adopted without objection, 23 November 1967.

Expresses its appreciation to the Review Team and to the Director-General for their report and recommendations (document CL 49/16);

Concurs in the need for organizational improvements in FAO so that it can be better able to meet its increasing responsibilities to the peoples of the world in the field of food and agriculture, particularly in the developing countries, and so that the Organization can continue to give increasingly efficient and practical assistance with qualified personnel having full understanding of the aspirations and the realities of those countries, as well as knowledge and competence in their respective fields;

Decides to move forward with the appointment of full-time Country Representative, chiefly financed from the UNDP, with over-all responsibility for FAO programmes within their respective countries;

Requests the Director-General within the approved budget for the biennium 1968/69 to proceed as rapidly as possible to expand the corps of Country Representatives in cooperation with the UNDP and to strengthen their effectiveness and responsibility in developing and carrying out the field programmes in their respective countries;

. . .

C. United Nations Educational, Scientific and Cultural Organization (UNESCO)

1. Constitution[1]

The Governments of the States Parties to this Constitution on behalf of their peoples declare:

That since wars begin in the minds of men, it is in the minds of men that the defences of peace must be constructed;

That ignorance of each other's ways and lives has been a common cause, throughout the history of mankind, of that suspicion and mistrust between the peoples of the world through which their differences have all too often broken into war;

. . .

For these reasons, the States Parties to this Constitution, believing in full and equal opportunities, for education for all, in the unrestricted pursuit of objective truth, and in the free exchange of ideas and knowledge, are agreed and determined to develop and to increase the means of communication between their peoples and to employ these means for the purposes of mutual understanding and a truer and more perfect knowledge of each other's lives;

In consequence whereof they do hereby create the United Nations Educational, Scientific and Cultural Organization for the purpose of ad-

---

[1]Adopted in London on 16 November 1945 and amended by the General Conference at subsequent sessions.

vancing, through the educational and scientific and cultural relations of the peoples of the world the objectives of international peace and of the common welfare of mankind, the objectives of international peace and of the common welfare of mankind for which the United Nations Organization was established and which its Charter proclaims.

Article I.

Purposes and Functions.

1. The purpose of the Organization is to contribute to peace and security by promoting collaboration among the nations through education, science and culture in order to further universal respect for justice, for the rule of law and for the human rights and fundamental freedoms which are affirmed for the peoples of the world, without distinction of race, sex, language or religion, by the Charter of the United Nations.

2. To realize this purpose the Organization will:

(a) Collaborate in the work of advancing the mutual knowledge and understanding of peoples, through all means of mass communication and to that end recommend such international agreements as may be necessary to promote the free flow of ideas by word and image;

(b) Give fresh impulse to popular education and to the spread of culture;

By collaborating with Members, at their request, in the development of educational activities;

By instituting collaboration among the nations to advance the ideal of equality of educational opportunity without regard to race, sex or any distinctions, economic or social;

By suggesting educational methods best suited to prepare the children of the world for the responsibilities of freedom;

(c) Maintain, increase and diffuse knowledge;

. . .

By encouraging co-operation among the nations in all branches of intellectual activity, including the international exchange of persons active in the fields of education, science and culture and the exchange of publications, objects of artistic and scientific interest and other materials of information;

By initiating methods of international cooperation calculated to give the people of all countries access to the printed and published materials produced by any of them.

3. With a view to preserving the independence, integrity and fruitful diversity of the cultures and educational systems of the States Members of the Organization, the Organization is prohibited from intervening in matters which are essentiaaly within their domestic jurisdiction.

. . .

198

2. EDUCATION AND EVOLUTION OF POPULATION:
RESOLUTION 14.C 3.252 (1966)

The Director-General is authorized, in co-operation with the competent international, regional and national governmental and non-governmental organizations, to stimulate and provide assistance towards scientific studies concerning the relations between the development of education and evolution of population, it being understood that this project will have a duration not exceeding 10 years, . . .

3. BROAD PERSPECTIVES FOR UNESCO ACTION IN THE POPULATION
FIELD: EXECUTIVE Board Resolution 77 EX/4.4.1 (1967)

The Executive Board,

1. *Recalling* resolution 3.252 concerning education and the evolution of population and the accompanying work plan adopted by the General Conference at its fourteenth session,
2. *Noting* resolution 1219 (XLIII) of the forty-third session of the Economic and Social Council, on the Development of Activities in the Field of Population, according to which, in particular:
"The Economic and Social Council
Urges all organizations within the United Nations system to make every effort within their competence designed to develop and render more effective their programmes in the field of population, including training, research, information and advisory services; and in particular *invites* Unesco to pursue actively its education, social sciences and mass media activities in this regard",
3. *Recognizing* the responsibilities in this field which are carried by the other organizations of the United Nations system and the need for coordination of activities,
4. *Having discussed* the Director-General's proposals on Unesco's responsibilities in the field of population prepared on the basis of the recommendations of a committee of experts (77 EX/13),
5. *Endorses* the broad perspectives put forward by the Director-General for the next ten years in regard to Unesco's action, as part of the coordinated United Nations programme in the field of population;
6. *Approves* in general, and in the light of the comments made by Members of the Board, the scope and main features of the Draft Programme for the years 1969-1972 set forth by the Director-General, taking into account, in particular, his recommendations concerning the role of Unesco as regards undertaking social science research and postponing the possible establishment of clearing house services in the field of population problems.

4. POPULATION AND FAMILY PLANNING:
   RESOLUTION 15C/1.241 (1968)

The General Conference,

Bearing in mind the resolution on human rights aspects of family planning, adopted on 12 May 1968 at the International Conference on Human Rights in Teheran,

. . .

Recalling further that in particular Unesco was invited to pursue actively its education, social sciences and mass media activities in this regard, and

Recalling the decision by the Executive Board at its 77th session concerning the development of a ten-year programme for collecting and encouraging the exchange of information on the inclusion of instruction on population questions in school curricula, as well as a programme for encouraging and assisting national mass communication agencies to develop their resources with a view to informing the public about population matters,

Noting the establishment of a Working Group on Population composed of representatives of the Secretariats of the United Nations, ILO, FAO, Unesco, WHO and Unicef,

Convinced that such close co-operation is of the utmost importance in programming population activities because of the multidisciplinary character of these subjects, and that coordination should be extended to include non-governmental organizations such as the International Planned Parenthood Federation (IPPF) and the International Union for the Scientific Study of Population, as well as bilateral programmes of cooperation,

Conscious of the need for including instruction on population questions in school courses, of expanding the opportunities for training of teachers and communication personnel in this field, of including family planning in all relevant curricula, and of developing technical manual on the application of communication methods in family planning programmes, stressing the necessity that all these forms of instruction should lay special emphasis on the socio-cultural implications of these activities,

Noting with satisfaction that, in 1969-1970, assistance will be given to Member States, at their request, under the Programme of Participation in Member States' Activities, in planning and conducting their activities in the fields of population and family planning and, in particular, to Member States in Asia with respect to the planning and use of mass media for national population and family planning programmes,

1. *Declares* that the purpose of Unesco's activities in the field of population should be to promote a better understanding of the serious responsibilities which population growth imposes on individuals, nations and

the whole international community, in the context of respect for human rights, the people's ethical convictions, the needs of Member States for development and the promotion of international cooperation,

2. *Considers*, therefore, that Unesco should act with due regard to the diversity of national situations and thus avoid any tendency to adopt uniform policies and procedures in regard to population policy and family planning,

3. *Invites* the Director-General:

(a) to further cooperation with other international governmental or non-governmental organizations by offering the services of Unesco within the fields of population and family planning with special emphasis on the socio-cultural implications thereof,

(b) to avoid any overlapping activities with other United Nations bodies,

4. *Authorizes* the Director-General to receive from Member States and the appropriate international organizations all possible voluntary aid in the form of specific financial contributions and the services of experts in Unesco's areas of work,

5. *Invites* the Director-General to continue his endeavour to render all possible assistance by Unesco to Member States in the fields of population and family planning which come within its competence,

6. *Instructs* the Director-General to prepare the Secretariat to meet in a coordinated manner the urgent demands from Member States within the fields of population and family planning:

(a) within Education:

(i) by helping in the development of teaching materials, curricula, teacher training, adult education, women's education, community education, etc.;

(ii) by studying the possibilities of including an educational pilot project on family planning in the experimental literacy programme;

(b) within Social Sciences by carrying out studies on the different aspects of population and family planning, so as to establish the intellectual base for understanding the complexity of family planning in the context of various cultures;

(c) within Communication:

(i) by studying ways for the establishment and operation of efficient programmes within the fields of population and family planning;

(ii) by providing relevant information and documentation.

5. APPLICATION OF THE SOCIAL SCIENCES TO HUMAN ENVIRONMENT AND POPULATION PROBLEMS: RESOLUTION 16C/3.25 (1970)

3.25 The Director-General is authroized to promote and assist the application of the social sciences to the problems of the human environment and human population:

(a) by examining man's role in changing his environment;

(b) by stimulating and assisting scientific studies on:

(i) the relations between the development of education and the evolution of population;

(ii) the interrelationship between psychological and cultural factors and birth control;

(c) by participating, at their request, in the activities of Member States concerned with problems relating to human environment and human population, within the framework of the programme of the Organization.

6. MASS MEDIA IN OUT-OF-SCHOOL EDUCATION:
   RESOLUTION 16C/4.24 (1970)

The Director-General is authorized:

(a) to undertake research and studies on the role of the media of mass communication in the education of youth and adults, and in particular on their use in literacy and family-planning campaigns;

(b) to undertake pilot projects and to organize seminars and training courses for the testing and demonstration of new methods in the use of mass communication in out-of-school education;

(c) to assist Member States, at their request, in developing the use of the mass media for out-of-school education.

7. POPULATION AND FAMILY PLANNING:
   RESOLUTION 16C/7.25 (1970)

The General Conference,

Bearing in mind Unesco's fundamental commitment to the dignity of man and the fact that the ultimate objective of development is the well-being of man,

Authorizes the Director-General to include in the future draft programmes activities relating to population and family planning to be carried out within the competence of Unesco and in cooperation with other competent international organizations, which would aim at:

(a) assisting Member States, on request, in the elaboration of population and family planning policies whose principles they have adopted in the full exercise of their rights and responsibilities;

(b) executing integrated studies based on existing knowledge of demographic situations of regions or countries in order to make available to Member States data regarding the highly complex differences in various demographic situations, with reference to the equally complex interaction between demographic evolution and education, science and culture, and thereby help in creating better understanding between countries of the various problems and approaches involved;

(c) setting up a programme of studies on the interrelationships between population development and the human rights directly affecting population.

8. POPULATION: RESOLUTION 17C/7.4 (1972)

The General Conference,

Recalling resolution 7.25 adopted at its sixteenth session,

Recalling decision 4.4.1 adopted by the Executive Board at its 77th session concerning the establishment and development of a ten-year programme for collecting and encouraging the exchange of information on the inclusion of instruction on population questions in school curricula, as well as a programme for encouraging and assisting national mass communication agencies to develop their activities with a view to informing the public about population matters,

Conscious of the urgent need for including instruction on population questions in the educational systems of Member States,

Recommends that the Director-General, co-operating in the Organization's fields of competence with the other competent institutions of the United Nations System as well as other international organizations, and using the funds from international and national sources available to him for this programme, with due regard for human rights and bearing in mind the diversity of cultures:

(a) establish the proper administrative framework, at an appropriate senior level within the Secretariat, for carrying out Unesco's activities in the field of population and family planning in conformity with the policies of Member States;

(b) undertake and encourage studies and research which will lead to a wider and deeper understanding of population and family planning problems and particularly of the motivation and consequences of human behaviour in this respect, and which will therefore help in the preparation of national policies and programmes in this area;

(c) undertake or encourage scientific studies of the possibilities offered by a better exploitation of the earth's resources as a factor in dealing with the problems of population growth;

(d) promote, by means of education and information, a clearer insight among the public into the nature, causes and consequences of demographic trends;

(e) inform Member States as soon as possible of the type of assistance which Unesco is now in a position to provide in the field of population and family planning, using, in particular, the opportunity provided by the presence of permanent representatives of Member States at Headquarters;

(f) assist Member States, on request, in the implementation of their national programmes for study, research, education and information in the area of population problems.

D. World Health Organization (WHO)

1. Constitution of the World Health Organization[1]

The States parties to this Constitution declare, in conformity with the Charter of the United Nations, that the following principles are basic to the happiness, harmonious relations and security of all peoples:

Health is a state of complete physical, mental and social well-being and not merely the absence of disease or infirmity.

The enjoyment of the highest attainable standard of health is one of the fundamental rights of every human being without distinction of race, religion, political belief, economic or social condition.

The health of all peoples is fundamental to the attainment of peace and security and is dependent upon the fullest cooperation of individuals and States.

The achievement of any State in the promotion and protection of health is of value to all.

Unequal development in different countries in the promotion of health and control of disease, especially communicable disease, is a common danger.

Healthy development of the child is of basic importance; the ability to live harmoniously in a changing total environment is essential to such development.

The extension to all peoples of the benefits of medical, psychological and related knowledge is essential to the fullest attainment of health.

Informed opinion and active cooperation on the part of the public are of the utmost importance in the improvement of the health of the people.

Governments have a responsibility for the health of their peoples which can be fulfilled only by the provision of adequate health and social measures.

Accepting These Principles, and for the purpose of cooperation among themselves and with others to promote and protect the health of all peoples, the contracting parties agree to the present Constitution and hereby

---

[1]Adopted by the International Health Conference held in New York from 19 June to 22 July 1946 and signed on 22 July 1946 by the representatives of 61 States. Amendments adopted by the Twelfth World Health Assembly came into force on 25 October 1960.

establish the World Health Organization as a specialized agency within the terms of Article 57 of the Charter of the United Nations.

CHAPTER I — OBJECTIVE

Article 1

The objective of the World Health Organization (hereinafter called the Organization) shall be the attainment by all peoples of the highest possible level of health.

CHAPTER II — FUNCTIONS

Article 2

In order to achieve its objective, the functions of the Organization shall be:

(a) to act as the directing and coordinating authority on international health work;

(b) to establish and maintain effective collaboration with the United Nations, specialized agencies, governmental health administrations, professional groups and such other organizations as may be deemed appropriate;

(c) to assist Governments, upon request, in strengthening health services;

(d) to furnish appropriate technical assistance and, in emergencies, necessary aid upon the request or acceptance of Governments;

. . .

(f) to establish and maintain such administrative and technical services as may be required, including epidemiological and statistical services;

. . .

(i) to promote, in cooperation with other specialized agencies where necessary, the improvement of nutrition, housing, sanitation, recreation, economic or working conditions and other aspects of environmental hygiene;

(j) to promote cooperation among scientific and professional groups which contribute to the advancement of health,

(k) to propose conventions, agreements and regulations, and make recommendations with respect to international health matters and to perform such duties as may be assigned thereby to the Organization and are consistent with its objective;

(l) to promote maternal and child health and welfare and to foster the ability to live harmoniously in a changing total environment;

(m) to foster activities in the field of mental health, especially those affecting the harmony of human relations;

(n) to promote and conduct research in the field of health;

(o) to promote improved standards of teaching and training in the health, medical and related professions;

(p) to study and report on, in cooperation with other specialized agencies where necessary, administrative and social techniques affecting public health and medical care from preventive and curative points of view, including hospital services and social security;

(q) to provide information, counsel and assistance in the field of health;

(r) to assist in developing an informed public opinion among all peoples on matters of health;

. . .

(u) to develop, establish and promote international standards with respect to food, biological, pharmaceutical and similar products;

(v) generally to take all necessary action to attain the objective of the Organization.

. . .

2. MATERNAL AND CHILD HEALTH: RESOLUTION WHA 1.42[1]

The First World Health Assembly

RESOLVES

(1) that the Executive Board be instructed to establish an expert committee to be called "The Expert Committee on Maternal and Child Health of the World Health Organization", with the following terms of reference:

To act as an advisory body to the World Health Organization;

(2) that the World Health Organization set up within its Secretariat a section on maternal and child health.

3. MATERNAL AND CHILD HEALTH: RESOLUTION WHA 1.43[2]

Whereas it is considered that the children of today represent the whole future of humanity and that maternal and child health is a problem of primary importance,

The First World Health Assembly

RECOMMENDS that Governments take -- subject to the conditions in their countries -- preventive, curative, legislative, social and other measures necessary for the protection of the health of mothers before, during, and after confinement, as well as for the welfare and upbringing of children, drawing special attention to:

---

[1]Adopted July 1948.
[2]Adopted July 1948.

(i) the protection of the health of adolescents -- particularly girls -- and expectant and nursing mothers who are employed in gainful occupations, and the prohibition of the gainful employment of children;

(ii) introduction of leave of absence for expectant mothers and leave after the birth of the child, with the continuation for the duration of leave of adequate wages;

(iii) access to adequate attendance for mothers during the birth of the child, both at home and in the hospital, especially for artificially aided births;

(iv) the organization of non-governmental and governmental institutions where adequate medical consultation on pregnancy hygiene and on feeding, care, and upbringing of children can be made accessible to families.

The World Health Organization should, through the maternal and child health and other sections:

(i) help to give effect to recommendations made by the Expert Committee and approved by the Executive Board on matters of maternal and child health;

(ii) give appropriate assistance to States with the agreement and on the request of the Governments concerned, on matters concerning investigation and lowering of maternal and infant mortality and maternal and child health services; and

(iii) collect and disseminate information on maternal and child health, acting as an international co-ordinating centre for activities for the benefit of mother and child.

4. HUMAN REPRODUCTION: RESOLUTION WHA 18.49[1]

The Eighteenth World Health Assembly,

Having considered the report of the Director-General on programme activities in the health aspects of world population which might be developed by WHO,

Bearing in mind Article 2 (1) of the Constitution which reads: "In order to achieve its objective, the functions of the Organization shall be . . . to promote maternal and child health and welfare and to foster the ability to live harmoniously in a changing total environment";

Noting resolution 1048 (XXVII) adopted by the Economic and Social Council at its thirty-seventh session, in August 1964;

Believing that demographic problems require the consideration of economic, social, cultural, psychological and health factors in their proper perspective;

---

[1]Adopted with no objection, 21 May 1965.

Noting that the United Nations Population Commission at its thirteenth session, in April 1965, attached high priority to the research and other activities in the field of fertility;

Considering that the changes in the size and structure of the population have repercussions on health conditions;

Recognizing that problems of human reproduction involve the family unit as well as society as a whole, and that the size of the family should be the free choice of each individual family;

Bearing in mind that it is a matter for national administrations to decide whether and to what extent they should support the provision of information and services to their people on the health aspects of human reproduction;

Accepting that it is not the responsibility of WHO to endorse or promote any particular population policy; and

Noting that the scientific knowledge with regard to the biology of human reproduction and the medical aspects of fertility control is insufficient,

1. APPROVES the report of the Director-General on programme activities in the health aspects of world population which might be developed by WHO;

2. REQUESTS the Director-General to develop further the programme proposed:

(a) in the fields of reference services, studies on medical aspects of sterility and fertility control methods and health aspects of population dynamics; and

(b) in the field of advisory services as outlined in Part III, paragraph 3, of his report, on the understanding that such services are related, within the responsibilities of WHO, to technical advice on the health aspects of human reproduction and should not involve operational activities; and

3. REQUESTS the Director-General to report to the Nineteenth World Health Assembly on the programme of WHO in the field of human reproduction.

5. Human Reproduction: Resolution WHA 19.43[1]

The Nineteenth World Health Assembly,

. . .

Noting the part played by economic, social and cultural conditions in solving population problems, and emphasizing the importance of health aspects of this problem;

Noting resolution 1084 (XXXIX) of the Economic and Social Council, the discussions at the Second World Population Conference and the sub-

---

[1] Adopted with no objection, 20 May 1966.

sequent discussion during the twentieth session of the United Nations General Assembly;

Noting that several Governments are embarking on nation-wide schemes of family planning;

Noting that the activities of WHO and its scientific groups have already played their part in collecting and making available information on many aspects of human reproduction;

Recognizing that the scientific knowledge with regard to human reproduction is still insufficient; and

Realizing the importance of including information on the health aspects of population problems in the education of medical students, nurses, midwives and other members of the health team,

. . .

4. CONFIRMS that the role of WHO is to give Members technical advice, upon request, in the development of activities in family planning, as part of an organized health service, without impairing its normal preventive and curative functions; and

5. REQUESTS the Director-General to report to the Twentieth World Health Assembly on the work of WHO in the field of human reproduction.

6. HUMAN REPRODUCTION: RESOLUTION WHA 20.41[1]

The Twentieth World Health Assembly,

Having considered the report of the Director-General on health aspects of population dynamics;

Welcoming particularly the references therein to provision of training;

Recognizing the urgent nature of the health problems associated with changes in population dynamics now facing certain Member States, especially in the recruitment of suitably trained and experienced staff;

. . .

Considering that abortions and the high maternal and child mortality rates constitute a serious public health problem in many countries; and

Believing that the development of basic health services is of fundamental importance in any health programme aimed at health problems associated with population,

. . .

4. REQUESTS the Director-General:

(a) to continue to develop the activities of the World Health Organization in the field of health aspects of human reproduction;

(b) to assist on request in national research projects and in securing the training of university teachers and of professional staff; and

[1]Adopted with no objection, 25 May 1967.

(c) to report to the Twenty-first World Health Assembly on the work of WHO in the field of human reproduction.

7. HUMAN REPRODUCTION: RESOLUTION WHA 21.43[1]

The Twenty-first World Health Assembly,

Recognizing that family planning is viewed by many Member States as an important component of basic health services, particularly of maternal and child health, and in the promotion of family health, and plays a role in social and economic development;

Reiterating the opinion that every family should have the opportunity of obtaining information and advice on problems connected with family planning, including fertility and sterility; and

Agreeing that our understanding of numerous problems related to the health aspects of human reproduction, family planning and population is still limited,

. . .

3. REQUESTS the Director-General:

(a) to continue to develop the programme in this field in accordance with the principles laid down in resolutions WHA 18.49, WHA 19.43 and WHA 20.41 including also the encouragement of research on psychological factors related to the health aspects of human reproduction;

(b) to continue to assist Member States upon their request in the development of their programmes with special reference to:

(i) the integration of family planning within basic health services without prejudice to the preventive and curative activities which normally are the responsibility of those services;

(ii) appropriate training programmes for health professionals at all levels;

(c) to analyse further the health manpower requirements for such services and the supervision and training needs of such manpower in actual field situations under specific local conditions; and

(d) to report on the progress of the programme to the Twenty-second World Health Assembly.

8. HUMAN REPRODUCTION: RESOLUTION WHA 22:32[2]

The Twenty-second World Health Assembly,

. . .

Emphasizing the primary importance of social and economic factors for the solution of these problems;

---

[1]Adopted with no objection, 23 May 1968.
[2]Adopted with no objection, 23 July 1969.

Reiterating the conviction that medicine and public health have substantial contributions to make in relation to these problems; and

Reaffirming the importance of an infrastructure of health services as the basis of all health services, including family planning,

. . .

3. REQUESTS the Director-General:

(a) to continue to develop the programme of advisory services, training, research and reference in this field in the direction undertaken;

(b) to evaluate various approaches to the introduction and development of services for family planning care specifically in the context of health services and generally in the context of community, economic and national development; and

(c) to continue to intensify the development of basic health services as the framework for meeting health needs, including family planning in those countries where this is necessary.

E.   International Bank for
Reconstruction and Development (IBRD)

1.   Articles of Agreement of the International Bank
for Reconstruction and Development[1]

Article I

Purposes

The purposes of the Bank are:

(i) To assist in the reconstruction and development of territories of members by facilitating the investment of capital for productive purposes, including the restoration of economies destroyed or disrupted by war, the reconversion of productive facilities to peacetime needs and the encouragement of the development of productive facilities and resources in less developed countries.

. . .

(iii) To promote the long-range balanced growth of international trade and the maintenance of equilibrium in balances of payments by encouraging international investment for the development of the productive resources of members, thereby assisting in raising productivity, the standard of living and conditions of labour in their territories.

(iv) To arrange the loans made or guaranteed by it in relation to international loans through other channels so that the more useful and urgent projects, large and small alike, will be dealt with first.

. . .

---

[1]Signed at Washington and came into force by acceptance, 27 December 1945.

The Bank shall be guided in all its decisions by the purposes set forth above.

. . .

2.   POPULATION PLANNING, SECTOR WORKING PAPER.[1]

"This paper describes the Bank's efforts to help member countries reduce population growth rates and sets out its future programme of activity in the field, as now envisaged.

"To give perspective to this discussion, the paper also outlines the economic effects of reducing population growth in developing countries and summarizes available information on the global demographic situation, world population trends and projections, and the accomplishments and potential of family planning programmes."[1]

---

[1]Population Planning, Sector Working Paper, World Bank, March 1972.